GREAT
MOMENTS
IN GOLF

GREAT MOMENTS IN GOLF

by Dave Klein

COWLES BOOK COMPANY, INC.

NEW YORK

Contents

Introduction

IT WAS A FOURTEEN-FOOT PUTT.

The ball curved and snaked its way across a green so smooth and so manicured it could have passed for carpet. It moved slowly, as befit its regal place in the history of the game of golf. And as it neared the lip of the cup, it seemed to hang for an instant, and no doubt the hearts of all who watched, hypnotized, must have stopped for just the wink of an eye.

And then it fell true.

And with the fall, a veteran touring golf pro named Bobby Nichols, on August 30, 1970, on the eighteenth green of the Upper Montclair Country Club in Clifton, New Jersey, earned a first prize of $60,000—more money than any pro golfer had ever won in any single previous tournament; indeed, it was more than any pro athlete, save a few of the storied heavyweight champions, had ever taken home for one performance.

It was the finale of the $300,000 Dow Jones Open, and it had been the inaugural of this world's richest tournament. It had offered more cash for second place ($34,200) and for third place ($21,300) than most events pay their winners. It staggered the imaginations of television viewers across the country. It excited the ambitions of future golf greats, the kids in their teens who watched and envied and dreamed. It boggled the minds of the club hack and the Sunday duffer and the dentist playing hooky. The money had, finally, become the means and the end in pro golf.

But no one would have been able to predict such richness for this game which induces a grown man to chase an elusive, small white ball over greens and pastures and up and down hills—then attempt to maim and disfigure it with a slender, weighted stick.

No one will ever be able to calculate accurately the winning potential of the early golfers, the ones named Francis Ouimet and Ted Ray, Harry Vardon and Willie Anderson, Walter Hagen and Bobby Jones and Gene Sarazen at their best. They lived at too early a time—a time when golf had not yet caught the fancy of the general public. They were accustomed to the quiet struggles that were part of the game, and took their own kind of joy from each small gain. Nevertheless, as golfers, they were unrecognized masters.

The life was hard and the rewards meager for these golfing pioneers, and it must have been the sheer lure of the sport, the challenge of this maddening game, that drove them on. They traveled the dirt roads of early America, playing where they could and when they could and whichever opponents were available, frequently playing for meal money and nothing more. Golfers were much the same as pro baseball players and pro football players in those early days—looked down on and sometimes considered shiftless, tawdry, without ambition or substance.

Then pro golf took off and skyrocketed. It sprouted the wings of Mercury and the touch of Midas, grabbed this nation by the nape of its neck and shook it, making it all worthwhile for the pioneers—at least, for those of them left to savor what they had wrought.

Perhaps the one man responsible was Arnold Palmer, but it is more likely that he was the first McLuhan-inspired electronic mass media hero. Blond, handsome, craggy and just country enough to be loved, he strode down from the foothills of Latrobe, Pennsylvania, and into the center of the golf boom. His dynamic, almost impossible charges on the final day of a tournament became patented, a part of the fabric of Americana, a measure of his mystique.

He unnerved his fellow pros and they faltered in the stretch when he was charging. He hit over trees rather than play safe; he hit over water and he dared the bunkers to claim his drives. He putted boldly and with daring, and he played fast, scorning the time-honored ritual of deliberate, slow maneuvers on the course.

Arnold Palmer became an international celebrity. He acquired charisma, the touch of folklore, the hint of gold. The television, advertising, and promotional people flew to him and made him a millionaire several times over.

Arnie's Army, those so-called huge galleries that followed his steps on each course he played, became as famous as the man for whom they cheered and wept and suffered, the man for whom they intimidated other pros by the sheer volume of their enthusiasm. And when the country's top sportswriters and news services chose to honor the decade that was the 1960's in sports they selected each sport's most outstanding athlete.

But then, not willing to settle for categories, they set out to find the ultimate champion, the best of the best. The Athlete of the Decade. And they swept past baseball's Willie Mays and basketball's Bill Russell and pro football's Johnny Unitas. They picked themselves Arnold Palmer. Surely, this single act alone speaks volumes for the acceptance and the popularity of the sport of golf.

Was it really Arnie who catapulted into public prominence and acceptance pro golf's tour of riches and heartbreak on the weekly installment plan? Or was it the almost-equal contributions of his contemporaries, such as Jack Nicklaus, Gary Player, and Billy Casper? Not really, not in the true sense of the search for origins. It was before that, well before their time. They took the game and they made it golden, but there were the others who fashioned and honed the game itself, who made it matter, who made it possible for Arnie and Jack and Gary.

There were many, and all had a hand in golf's growth. They all had to make their way anonymously at first until they became known and began to capture the imagination and interest of more and more of the people. Indeed, several became distinct personalities, and national sports figures.

A few of them were caught up by the particular madness of their decade. The Roaring Twenties had its golfing heroes, as did the Depression Thirties, the Wartime Forties, the Emerging Fifties and the Golden Sixties.

But whom shall we designate as the founder, the father? Whom shall we point to as the single individual most responsible for making golf click as a sport? No one, and yet everyone. The game itself created its own fame, but the men who played the game when it was new made it work, and so credit must go to all those who participated in the $100 tournaments, the driving contests, and the putting matches; to all those who puttered away in basements and garages to improve the quality and performance of the clubs, renovating the faces, redesigning the balances and providing the ultimate tools with which the power hitters boom and the precision chippers place their almost magical shots; to those who took personal risks to sponsor tournaments, put up prize money, publicize the sport, and browbeat sports editors to grant coverage to this emerging national pastime.

They all deserve credit for getting golf off the ground—or on better, greener, more stable ground, if you will.

But when such a movement had begun, certain tournaments had to acquire prestige, the creation of which would supply the sport with its own drama and excitement. For, even without the impetus and attraction of the big names and the hundreds of thousands of dollars waiting for the participants, there are certain tournaments that make heroes of their winners. They are the Masters, the PGA, the U.S. Open, and the British Open.

This, accordingly, is an entirely different aspect of golf: the tradition.

Today there are tournaments for nearly every state, as well as golf spectaculars named for and sponsored by nearly every giant corporation. Stars of stage and screen put up money for the honor of naming their own tournament.

Groups and Chambers of Commerce and fraternal organizations fight for the right to sponsor an approved tournament, and the tour itself now stretches clear around the calendar, moving with the seasons, following the good weather, the prize money, and the media exposure.

But without meaning to offend, who remembers, from year to year, the winner of the San Diego Open, or the Greensboro Open, or the Kemper Classic, or the Danny Thomas Classic? They are all lucrative and respectable, and attract their generous share of topflight performers. But the golfer who wins the PGA, the Masters, or one of the two great Opens, well, he has really made his future. The winning of one of these four tournaments adds a permanent luster to his name, no matter what other honors he may achieve. The effect is immediate and jolting, and the reputation is forever.

Thus, whatever else Ken Venturi may accomplish in golf, he will be remembered as "the man who won the 1964 Open." And no matter how the future goes for Orville Moody, he will always be "that old Army sergeant who won the 1969 Open." And the Grand Slam will always be the most spectacular achievement of Bobby Jones, winner of the British Amateur, the U.S. Amateur, the U.S. Open and the British Open, all in 1930.

The list of winners of these prestigious tournaments is filled with several golfing immortals. But it is also dotted more than just infrequently with the names of those who never won much else, but who are still remembered for winning the big one. Vic Ghezzi, Art Wall, Jr., Don January—they and scores like them are secure in the annals of golf, for they won The Big One.

But, for all intents and purposes, golf remained a rich man's sport, confined to private turf, to exclusive country club greens, until fairly recently. Then it was discovered by two crucial segments of modern life simultaneously: the general public and network television. That kicked golf into the upper reaches, and it increased the prize money because television was willing to subsidize the tour for the right to sell the time to sponsors, which, really, is what TV is all about.

Before the "revolution" in the game the top prize in a smaller regional tournament was usually $5,000, with the entire purse perhaps totaling $20,000 for all entrants. With the advent of TV that same tournament suddenly took on major proportions, offering $10,000 or better to the winner and $50,000 overall. Allocating money to the top forty or fifty finishers guaranteed richer players and more of them, as well as wider saturation.

Golf suddenly became big-time because of television. The sale of clubs, bags, balls, clothing, and other accouterment has zoomed since 1950. One sporting goods firm computes a 1,000 percent increase in the sale of clubs. Another company insists it has hiked the turnover of golf balls 4,500 percent in twenty years. Think of that!

Now the successful pros tour the country in their sleek cars or in private planes. They endorse commercial products for thousands of dollars in fees and royalties. They are paid to give others the privilege of playing a round with a real, true-to-life pro, the same man the wealthy club members watch on television. They are the companions of stars and politicians, held in awe by financiers and bankers, pursued by agents and business managers.

Today thousands of youngsters are already shooting in the

low 70's before their 15th birthday, the natural result of becoming infatuated with the sport at an early age. One day the regulars on the tour will be going around in the mid-to-low 60's, because the kids are coming up fast. Look at what the new breed of players did to basketball as the acceptance of that game grew.

They took the jump shot and made it a science, and now the pros are almost miraculously proficient, and are capable of scoring almost at will. The game has become a race to score the last goal, not the most. Look at what has happened in pro football. Realize, if you will, that a mere decade ago the middle linebacker of the New York Giants stood six feet tall and weighed 200 pounds; in 1970, he stood six-four and weighed in at 245. The earlier the kids latch onto the game, the better that game will become, the more demanding and the more specialized.

Golf will likely see further interesting developments in the next few years, when the first true crop of youngsters is ready to burn up courses.

In 1927, a tournament of the top touring pros was informally arranged for El Paso, Texas. It included Tommy Armour, Al Espinosa and Bobby Cruickshank. The prize money? It totaled $1,000. But later that year, in Los Angeles, a promoter decided something that would be called the Los Angeles Open was worth a total prize-money figure of $10,000. He nearly was trampled to death in the rush of golfers seeking to enter. A tournament with a similar amount of cash was played in 1930 in St. Paul, Minnesota. And the totals stayed that way, hovering between $1,000 and $5,000, until Fred Corcoran took over as tour director of the newly-formed Professional Golfers Association in 1936. Fred, a husky and robust promoter in his own right, went directly to work. Figures will show that the year he took over offered eight tour events worth between $3,000 and $10,000 in total prize money.

They were the Los Angeles Open ($10,000); the Oakland, San Francisco, Miami, St. Petersburg Opens and the Masters at Augusta ($5,000 each), and the St. Augustine and Houston Opens ($3,000 each).

The first $100,000 tournament was inaugurated in 1941, a scant five years later, when George S. May, an admirer of the sport, founded the All-American Tournament at Tam O'Shanter in Chicago.

And so the game has moved into the field of big business, because there are men who have not won a tournament outright in five years and yet have earned upwards of $75,000 a year with lower finishes. Where once they played for food money and a layer cake or a loving cup, they are now cutting strokes worth nearly $5,000 apiece in some instances. Calculate the difference between Bobby Nichols' 276, worth $60,000, and the 277 shot by Labron Harris, worth nearly $30,000 less, in the Dow Jones tournament.

But the prize money is only one aspect of the riches these modern tour golfers accrue. The winner of any one of the American Big Three—the Open, the PGA or the Masters —can parlay his championship into $1,000,000 with the aid of endorsements, personal appearances, and exhibitions. Palmer's success is not as unique as it might appear. He simply made more from equipment manufacturing under his own name, from a chain of putting courses and dry-cleaning establishments, from movie appearances, TV guest spots, and instructional syndication for the nation's newspapers.

The government has reaped a financial harvest from Arnie's golf success. It is reported he paid taxes on close to $1,000,000 in personal income for the last three years.

Even the young men who have graduated from the PGA school in Florida to earn their tour cards are not compelled to scrimp and save and cut expense corners as was the case with the early masters. The manufacturing companies are hungry for new talent, fresh faces, and they will sign the beginners to lucrative contracts as endorsees, hoping one will make it big, crack open the magic bubble, and become another Palmer or Nicklaus.

Finally, with the golf boom already a clear and present reality, with the decreasing scores making it more difficult to even stay close by shooting par on the toughest courses in the world, there will come a day when the young ones scoff at the scores Palmer carded in building his empire. "He shot 280 and won? He'd be twenty strokes behind us now."

CHAPTER ONE

Ouimet Defeats Vardon and Ray in 1913 U.S. Open Playoff

PICTURE, IF YOU WILL, THE GLAMOR SURROUNDING A MAJOR star of any sport. The awe such men evoke from beginners is often accompanied by trembling, quaking knees, and cold, clammy palms. The rookie meets Willie Mays and is suddenly tongue-tied; the young quarterback encounters John Unitas and in an instant makes himself sound like a little child; the schoolboy star meets Wilt Chamberlain or Willis Reed and temporarily forgets all he knows about the game of basketball.

A new member of the touring pros has only to meet a Palmer or a Nicklaus to start the "sirs" and "misters" flying as fast as the stuttered words of praise. The truly outstanding athletes do touch off such reactions from younger men, be they fans or participants in the same game. Such men are somehow set apart from the rest—protected and gifted and flawless, wrapped in a spotless, shining, gleaming image. One does not converse with them as with mere mortals, much less harbor secret thoughts of reaching them or beating them at their game.

Such was the classic hero-worship syndrome of a young man in 1913 when he was brought face-to-face with the two most storied golfers in the world—Britishers Harry Vardon and Ted Ray.

The boy was twenty and rather gangly and gawky, the son of an immigrant gardener who lived down the road and across the pasture from the haughty and prestigious The Country Club in Brookline, Massachusetts. He was also an entrant in the U.S. Open, a fact that puzzled his father and worried his mother. The father could not understand the fatal attraction to golf, considering it a game for the idle rich. The mother fretted that her frail, thin son would tire trudging up and down the hills and across the wide fields of The Country Club's course.

The boy had become enamored with golf years earlier, and had, indeed, caddied the course for 28 cents an hour, meanwhile learning club selection, the lie of the fairways, and the reading of the greens. His name was Francis Ouimet, and he was going to make history. He was going to jolt the world of golf.

In 1913, golf was still a continental game, and its superiority was controlled by the British, the Scots and the French. There were some top Americans, but they were not yet in the class with the world's best, and the U.S. Open, which was that year awarded to The Country Club for the first time, figured to be an international triumph for one of the two Englishmen—Vardon, the artist, the shot-maker, or Ray, the muscleman, the monstrous driver who conquered courses with brute strength, shunning finesse.

Perhaps, it was felt, one of the more accomplished Americans, such as Johnny McDermott or Tom McNamara, would give the Britishers a battle. Another Londoner, Wilfred Reid, and perhaps a Frenchman, Louis Tellier, had outside chances. But no one expected Vardon and Ray to be beaten. It was believed they would go to the wire together, fighting in titanic, epic grandeur. The Americans were simply hoping for a representative showing from their group.

No one expected Vardon and Ray to be beaten—particularly not by a fuzz-faced boy who addressed them as Mr. Vardon and Mr. Ray and did so in a voice marked by a pronounced quaver.

Yet golf was Ouimet's game, too, as much as it was Vardon's and Ray's. He knew this Brookline course as well as he knew the towering reputations of the men he was going to meet, and of course that proved to be a great asset. It gave him an edge of considerable import for those moments when he was faced with a long putt or a difficult lie in the crucible-hot pressure of the competition. Golf was Ouimet's game but only he realized it then. The world knew only that Vardon and Ray had crossed the ocean to win.

And so Francis Ouimet ("Frankie" to his friends), a boy with too-big ears and sunken cheeks and a tentative, almost apologetic grin, began to play his game.

He drove not for distance but for accuracy, because he knew the perils of trying to out-muscle this giant of a course. He pitched not for the roll but for the hit, since he knew the greens were tricky-fast, and too much overspin would leave him with horrendously long putts. He knew how to contend with a wet, windy weather situation which rendered the fairways slick and the greens absolutely glass-like.

Most of all, Francis Ouimet was able to play quietly, almost unnoticed in the glare of the international stars gracing the greens. He and another young American, a twenty-year-old from Rochester, New York named Walter Hagen, attracted absolutely no early attention. Ouimet performed with a methodical determination that was to mark his entire career. He never took a chance he considered to be unwarranted. He played conservative, cautious golf, driving straight and true, pitching clean and high, putting slowly and with deliberation.

Meanwhile, the heroes were beating the course or the course was beating the heroes, and at the end of 36 holes Vardon was out there at 147, on top but tied with Reid for the lead. Vardon, ever the stylist, had mastered the course from the outset. He read the greens correctly and he noted the configuration of the fairways, and chose to hit high and soft. He finessed the field, and very nearly captivated the gallery at his heels with his craftsmanship. Reid? It was thought that Reid was a fine performer who was playing noble golf, but everyone saw that Vardon had his game going and so, of course, Reid had no chance.

The other half of this feared duo, Ray, was at 149, just

two strokes back despite several holes played with the grace of a bull elephant. But his incredible driving ability, his strength on the course, pulled him out of danger time after time, and while he was scrambling, he was, nevertheless, there. He was two strokes back and charging like a primeval Palmer.

Ouimet? He shot a credible 151 for the first 36. So did Hagen. The rest were nowhere.

Then, on the third round, Vardon skied just a trifle and came in with 78. Ray shot a 76 and earned the expected third-round tie with his countryman. But they turned around after the eighteenth and read the scorecards for the other competitors and found the young American, Ouimet, had come in with a solid 74. They had been tied by a boy of twenty.

But after all, a tie after three rounds is a gulf away from the championship. Vardon and Ray, veterans of many such pressure tournaments, realized this quickly. Both had been in similar situations often enough. When the pressure rose yet another impossible notch, when the withheld breath of the galleries could be felt as though an iron band restricted breathing, then the wisp of a lad would break and crack, his game would crumble, and he would later murmur congratulations to the winner, mumble thanks for giving him a lifetime thrill.

Right? Wrong.

The fourth round was again played under sloppy conditions, as persistent rain slowed the course, puddled the fairways, and turned the greens soggy. Vardon shot a final-round 79 to close the four-round scoring at 304. Ray, muttering oaths at the weather and the thick rough in which he often found himself, also trudged back with a 79. They were tied, and the boy was still on the course. The boy was playing his game, while the two stars had finished theirs.

He was playing consistent and methodical golf. He approached the thirteenth needing two birdie holes on the final six—the rest pars—to forge the tie and force a three-way play-off. The hometown crowd was suddenly his. They cheered at his successes and moaned audibly at his failures. They were with him, for him. He was the neighborhood caddy suddenly thrust into the world's limelight. Could he do it?

Well, he took care of one of those two birdies he needed with great dispatch. He chipped into the hole from a point that was thirty feet from the flag.

Fourteen was parred, as were the following two holes. He was playing well and he was playing par golf, but now there were only two holes to go and one of them had to be birdied. The gallery held its nervous breathing in check as he teed up for the seventeenth.

It was a dogleg to the right, and Ouimet hit a good tee shot, on the main stem of the fairway within chipping distance of the green. He marched confidently after the ball, while his ten-year-old caddy, Eddie Lowery, whispered calming words of confidence:

"Take your time, Frankie. Hit it solid, Frankie. Don't rush it, Frankie. Make them wait for you."

Lowery was later to become a successful auto dealer in San Francisco and sponsor the start of the careers of Ken Venturi and Harvie Ward.

The approach shot was hit perfectly, but the spin did not take hold because of the wetness of the green, and the ball wound up twenty feet past the pin. It was a tough spot, for a par now would put absolute pressure on number eighteen. It would be then or never. Now was the time to put it away. But it was, after all, a twenty-footer, and on a wet, slippery, and suddenly not-reliable green.

As if understanding the impossibility of all he had done thus far, realizing that more than simply skill had gone into this classic striving for a shocking upset, Ouimet shrugged at the lie. "Twenty feet?" he said later. "It could have been two feet or two hundred. I was going to hit it the same way."

So he stroked it hard and quickly and watched. The ball never wavered. It sped down the green, holding to the grain of a sidehill direction, and dropped in. He had his birdie. Now for the par on eighteen and a triple tie. The kid was ready to make history. Indeed, as he later admitted, he could have won the tournament outright, but to go for the birdie on the par-four eighteenth would have been sheer folly.

And Frankie Ouimet never took chances.

The drive on eighteen was solid, straight, and true. The approach shot was never better, stopping near the front part of the green, just where he wanted it—"just where it had to be," he was to say. He chipped up to the green, five feet short of the cup. And there it was. The ball was five feet away from a par, five feet way from Harry Vardon and Ted Ray, five feet away from the impossible dream of a twenty-year-old amateur. It was five feet that would be recounted for years and years, regardless of how it ended.

The skinny boy walked up to the ball and wasted absolutely no time at all.

"It was a straight putt," he said later. "All I had to do was hit it. The way I was going, this was no time to start worrying."

He simply "hit it good" and it rolled directly to the back of the cup and dropped. There was no dramatic pause in mid-flight, no rimming of the cup while the world turned blue in the face. Just a nice, solid whack and a nice, reassuring thud as the ball hit the hole. Just the way he had done it countless other times on the very same green.

And so the tournament was tied, tied at 304 by Harry Vardon, the expected; by Ted Ray, the expected; and by Francis Ouimet, the totally unexpected, the upset-maker, the pride of a nation. The 18-hole playoff was scheduled for the next day. Now, surely, Ouimet would break. Now, after all this and still no championship, his game would crack. Surely, after playing the best golf he had ever played and still finding the ever-present Vardon and Ray even with him, he would crumble.

Not a chance.

The next morning broke gray and leaden, heavy with dampness. The ground was wet and soggy. It was raining when the three men took their places at the first tee. And it rained for the duration of the match, but the rain could not dampen the glory of Francis Ouimet that day, nor could it wash away the courage he showed in the face of intense pressure, a pressure perhaps not previously experienced by any golfer.

Through the first nine the three contestants were dead even. No one wavered, no one broke, no one lost his nerve to the tension. Not even the kid, and certainly not Harry Vardon or Ted Ray.

And then, finally, came the first indication that September 20, 1913, was going to make golf in these United States sing with pride and jubilation. On the tenth hole, with the two men and the boy locked in a death-grip tie, the men broke first. Vardon three-putted the tenth for a five. Then Ray did the same. Ouimet? Steady as ever, almost unaware of what he was doing, he parred the 140-yard hole. He was in front. He had the lead.

And he was not going to relinquish it.

Ray finally threw it in on the fifteenth. His booming drive rammed right into the gallery and struck a spectator. Then he had to take two shots to get out, pitched into a bunker and needed two blasts to come clear. He flailed away at the ball, settled for a double-bogey six, and was four shots behind Vardon, the stylist, and Ouimet, the kid.

At the seventeenth, where the day before Ouimet had made his classic twenty-foot putt, Vardon hooked into the thick grass that knotted the fringe of the fairway and played safe, knocking the ball onto the fairway before resuming his advance to the cup. He took a five. Ouimet, as calm as he had been to this point, serenely sank an eighteen-foot putt for a birdie-three, and now held a three-stroke lead over Vardon.

Ray was gone, floundering in the morass of the wetness and his own suddenly panicky drives. And Vardon was almost gone. He knew it, and on the final hole he blew up and carded a double-bogey six. He was broken, shaken. Ray managed one final burst of courage and came up with a birdie-three. And Ouimet, who was going to become the Open champion barring a remote last-minute collapse, still retained his unshakable poise.

He teed off remarkably well, belting his drive directly up the middle of the fairway. He approached to within eighteen feet of the pin and stroked a long, positional putt to within four feet. And then, as he studied the lie and the position he was in, he suddenly realized that he was going to win the championship.

"For the first time, I thought about it, and all of a sudden it was hard for me to catch my breath. I couldn't stop gasping. And the green started moving around on me, like waves. I didn't even see the cup when I putted."

But to the gallery, he seemed numb, as if mesmerized by the competition, the pressure. He stroked and the ball made a docile exit from view, entering the cup, giving Francis Ouimet the U.S. Open championship of 1913, and launching a career that, perhaps more than any other, brought golf out from the blue-blood set and into the world of the common man.

A paragraph in *The London Times* echoes the vast respect with which the English held Ouimet's victory. "There will never be another like it," the writer penned. "When we are old men, little golfing children will ask us to tell them again the romantic story."

Ouimet was to go on to great victories and to a satisfying career as an amateur of world-wide renown. But he would never equal the drama of his Open victory, and he would later admit it was the peak of his career, a career that did not end until the 1950's. His accomplishments were many, and they bear recounting.

To run quickly down the record, Ouimet's championships include, apart from the 1913 Open, the U.S. Amateur in 1914 and 1931; the French Amateur in 1914; membership on the United States Walker Cup team consecutively from 1922 through 1949, and the captaincy of that team from 1936 through 1949. He was elected as an original member of Golf's Hall of Fame in 1944.

In addition, he was runner-up in the U.S. Amateur once, in 1920; and semifinalist six times, in 1923, 1924, 1926, 1927, 1929, and 1932. His Walker Cup record includes four singles victories (against two defeats and two halvings). Foursomes of which he was a part won five and lost three matches.

But the impact with which he hit the country was far more significant. His was a meaningful contribution to a sport that was, for the United States, still in its infancy. He became a national hero with his Open championship and he remained the nation's single most recognized golfer for many years, and did not yield that honor even when others drew equal fame, such as Bobby Jones, Gene Sarazen, Chick Evans, Johnny Farrell, and Willie MacFarlane.

Ouimet's grip on British memory was equally strong, and in 1951 he became the first non-Briton to be named a captain of the Royal and Ancient Golf Club of St. Andrews in Scotland, said to be the birthplace of golf. And bedecked in the traditional red jacket, he teed off on that historic day while a crowd cheered his entrance. The honor was no ordinary gesture by the Scots. Previous captains included the Duke of Windsor (in 1922) and the King of England himself (in 1930).

Perhaps as interesting in this unique career is the fact that Francis Ouimet never abandoned his amateur standing. He was at least as good a golfer as any of the touring pros, and there were sufficient chances during his peak years to get in on the embryonic money matches.

Ouimet always considered golf a game of enjoyment and not to be pursued for income. Thus, had he been able to devote all his time and all his energies to the game, he might have racked up even more impressive honors. Actually, there is no way of estimating how good he might have been, for to conduct a full-time business and play golf only when it is feasible is no way to sharpen and maintain a competitive edge. The game must be played regularly, daily, as today's pros do it.

As a result of Ouimet's altruism, he never really made another serious run at the Open championship. He returned in 1914 as the defending champion and, at the age of 21, finished a credible fifth. But from 1914 until 1925 he did not enter the tournament, and when he did again, he tied for second with Farrell, one stroke behind Bobby Jones and Willie Mac-Farlane, who needed a playoff to settle their stalemate. That was Ouimet's final appearance in a U.S. Open tournament, and he spent the remaining amount of highly-competitive years as a member of the United States' Walker Cup team, participating in more of these matches than any other golfer.

To understand completely the motivation of the man with respect to his dogged refusal to leap in with the money-tour set, one must know the particular atmosphere in which he lived and, perhaps as important, the type of golf he was brought up to play. He was an amateur at heart, one who played for pleasure and not for profit.

Ouimet was born in Brookline, a surburban area of Boston, on May 8, 1893, and his family soon moved to the location opposite The Country Club. It was this act that started Francis Ouimet on his collision course with Vardon and Ray and the rest of the world's top golfers, for he and his brother Wilfred soon were accepted into the caddy corps at the tightly-restricted club.

There was a long-standing regulation at The Country Club that forbade the caddies from playing on the course, but as all boys will do, Francis and his brother stole brief moments of golf in the odd, off hours. Finally, having been totally absorbed by the game, he went to work as a part-time dry goods clerk to earn the entrance fees for the National Amateur of 1910, which was scheduled to be played that year in Brookline. He earned the cash but failed to qualify.

It was the same story in 1911 and 1912, when he tried without success to qualify for the Amateur. But in 1912 he began to edge out into the golfing firmament—at least locally—by going to the final of the State Amateur (in Massachusetts) before losing the title. He did not make the same mistake in his magical year of 1913, for when he again advanced to the final round of the Massachusetts State Amateur, he became the new champion. Later that year, of course, the title's importance diminished considerably with his victory in the U.S. Open.

It is a strange quirk of circumstances that, after acquiring the United States Open championship, signifying the best of the professionals as well as the amateurs, Francis Ouimet finally qualified for the U.S. Amateur—and was defeated. He reached the semifinals before Jerry Travers sent him home. But he won the first of his two U.S. Amateurs the next season at Manchester, Vermont, and gained a measure of satisfaction by dumping Travers in the final round, 6 up with 5 to go. That year, 1914, was the one in which he also gained the French Amateur mantle, his first international title.

His career was to parallel that of a younger man, Bobby Jones, and three times Ouimet was to fall before the "greatest amateur golfer who ever lived" in the semifinals of the U.S. Amateur. The quote was his own, for he respected Jones's playing ability greatly and this, coupled with a severe affliction of modesty, was how he spent his time, turning down praise for a chance to laud Jones instead.

Jones, who was an 11-year-old boy in Atlanta, Georgia, when Francis Ouimet, nine years older, was winning the U.S. Open, was later to become a close friend and friendly adversary of Ouimet's, and he has often remarked about the style with which Francis played golf.

"The man had a natural gift, a God-given ability to play this game," Jones has said. "I have often considered myself fortunate to have been able to play with him, fortunate to have known him and very fortunate, indeed, to have occasionally beaten him in matches. There was no finer man."

Ouimet died on September 2, 1967, mourned by all who had come to know this quiet, modest, unassuming man; mourned by all those who remembered the glory of his career; mourned by all those who, most of all, remembered the excitement that gripped a nation on September 19, 1913, when the slim, bashful young man strode the course of the haughty, The Country Club in Brookline, Massachusetts, and brought home a championship to a country just discovering the appeal of golf.

Perhaps the recollection of that day by the ten-year-old boy who caddied for Francis Ouimet, the future sponsor and United States Golf Association official Eddie Lowery, can capsulize the thrill for those who were there.

"Francis said he tried to get 'numb' because then he would not have to think about what he was doing. 'If I think about it,' he said, 'I know for sure something will go wrong.' When he won, when he had finally done it, he turned to me and said: 'Well, Eddie, I can think about it now, but I'm so excited I'm not sure what to think about.' "

The world of golf owes a great debt to Francis Ouimet. He took the game from the backyards of the rich and put it into the pastures of the everyday man.

CHAPTER TWO

Sarazen Defeats Hagen for the "World Championship" — 1922

IT MAY WELL BE TRUE THAT THE TWO MOST COLORFUL men to play the sport of golf in the first fifty years of the twentieth century did so during the same period, which extended roughly from 1913 through 1940, although both played beyond that date as well.

But it was during this span, which started with Walter Hagen and soon picked up Gene Sarazen, that golf became more than a game. It became an entertainment, a road show followed by millions, a flashy and colorful spectacle that provided vicarious kicks for Americans across the country.

Each man was brash and brassy, cocky and confident, and each exhibited no hesitation whatsoever in proclaiming himself as the most dominant and influential factor in the game, the finest golfer of the time. Indeed, each could have made a case for such statements—and each did.

Hagen—he was known as "The Immortal Haig"—won the U.S. Open in 1914 and 1919; the British Open in 1922, 1924, 1928 and 1929; the PGA in 1921 and then consecutively from 1924 through 1927; the French Open in 1920; the Belgian Open in 1924; the Canadian Open in 1931; Ryder Cup team captaincy in 1927, 1929, 1931, 1933, 1935, 1937 (when a rookie named Sam Snead made his first appearance on the team), and 1939; and, in the years of 1924, 1926, 1927, and 1928, the 72-hole playoffs that earned for him the title of Unofficial World's Champion.

Sarazen (born Eugene Saraceni) includes among his triumphs the National Open in 1922 and again in 1932; the British Open of 1932; the PGA in 1922, 1923 and 1933; the

Masters of 1935; the 1954 and 1958 PGA Seniors; Ryder Cup membership in 1927, 1929, 1931, 1933, 1935, and 1937; as well as the Unofficial World's Championship in 1922—at the age of twenty!

It was that championship of 1922 that provided golf with a truly outstanding moment of drama and excitement, for much as in Francis Ouimet's 1913 Open surprise, there was the element of youth challenging the establishment, the sort of approved arrogance that makes for headlines and fans.

There had been some early disputes between these two men, for despite Sarazen's impressive string of victories and obvious golfing skill, the haughty Hagen refused to acknowledge his position.

"He always called me 'kid'," Sarazen recalls, "and I just had to get him. I had to show him I was as good as he was. Trouble with that, though, is that only myself and a few friends really believed I was."

But after capturing both the Open and the PGA in 1922, and after beating two of the generally regarded "top three" golfers in the land (Jim Barnes and Jock Hutchinson), to earn the championships, Sarazen would settle for nothing less than Hagen.

"If he beat me, well, that would be my fault," Gene recalled. "But I had to see if he would . . . or could."

Spurred on by the curious public and by many prodding sportswriters, the challenge was made. Two rounds of 36 holes each would be played, on consecutive days and on different courses. The first day would be at Oakmont in Pittsburgh, a sprawling monster of a course with greens as treacherous as any in America. The second day would be spent at the old Westchester-Biltmore course in Rye, New York (now the Westchester Country Club). It was scheduled for Oct. 6-7, and the nation was anxiously awaiting the result. Would it be the young Turk or the old guard?

Weeks before it was to be held, The Haig began his customary psychological war, his battle of nerves to intimidate his opponent. He was famous for such practices. If he was irreverent, well, he had his own justification for that, too. "You're only here for a short visit," he once declared. "So don't hurry, don't worry, and be sure to smell the flowers along the way." He was flamboyant and caustic-tongued when he had to be, but mostly he enjoyed golf as a sport and was genuinely surprised that he had managed to make (and spend) as much as he did while having fun.

Friends have estimated that Haig frittered away more than a million dollars in winnings during his career. He was, for instance, a notoriously heavy tipper, flinging around large bills at waiters and hat check girls alike, part and parcel a true representative of the Roaring Twenties. He would frequently turn over his entire winning check to a particularly helpful or likeable caddy, and the clothes he ordered and wore became part of his legend.

He also was quick to take offense if he felt he was being slighted. When he arrived for the 1920 British Open, he found that the clubhouse at the posh and plushy Deal Club was "off limits" to professionals, at whom the British still sneered because they regarded them as mercenaries. He was, instead, dispatched in haste to the pro's shop, where he was told he could dress.

"Not me," roared The Haig, when he viewed the small, dingy and inadequate quarters.

So he ordered a long limousine, had it parked at the front gate of the country club daily, and changed in the car. And each day his chauffeur, who also doubled as a footman, met him at the eighteenth green with a fresh polo coat.

Thus Sarazen had hooked a giant. Two weeks before they were to meet, Hagen announced to the press that he had ordered two pairs of exclusively knitted hose for the contest, with "The Haig" sewn around the cuffs. It was typical of Hagen, as part of the intimidation strategy. Indeed, he would intimidate any way he could. He once called Mike Brady out of the clubhouse to have him watch Haig's final putt—which tied Brady for the lead at the conclusion of the fourth round of the 1919 Open at Brae Burn (Massachusetts). Then, as they teed off in the eighteen-hole playoff the next day, he calmly assayed Brady and said: "Mike, don't you think you should roll your sleeves down? You know, so the gallery won't see your muscles quiver."

Another time, in a crucial moment of a tournament, Hagen chipped to within fifteen feet of the cup while his opponent had come much closer, perhaps four to five feet away.

As they paused to consider their putting possibilities, Hagen suddenly burst out in a merry peal of laughter.

"What's so funny?" asked the suspicious opponent.

"Oh, I was just thinking," Hagen chuckled.

"About what?" asked the opponent.

"About how much harder your putt will look after I make mine."

Hagen then smacked at the ball and sank the putt; his unnerved opponent missed the closer one and lost the match.

But Sarazen was not to be outdone in any fashion. When the news of Hagen's new hose reached him, he ordered two new golf suits and told the press he would wear one at Oakmont, the other at Westchester-Biltmore, and then discard them. It was somewhat puzzling behavior from two such immortal golfing figures, but one must remember that in the early 1920's all America behaved like Gloria Swanson and other Hollywood celebrities.

Sarazen admits he hardly slept the night before the match was to begin, lying awake with stomach cramps, butterflies and "Hagen-itis." The fact that he and the Haig traveled together on the sleeper train to Oakmont might have had something to do with it, for they tried their hand at a little dice during the trip and Hagen won easily.

"Kid," he intoned, "I guess I'm going to be able to beat you at anything."

It was hardly an auspicious beginning nor, in fact, was the 36-hole first-round at Oakmont the next day. The Haig blissfully hit every ball properly and emerged from the first half of the challenge with a two-stroke lead. Sarazen had been down by four strokes at one point, and had also exhibited his bad case of nerves by missing five putts of less than five feet each.

So it was a disconsolate lad of twenty who entrained for Rye, New York, that night, seemingly on the way to a defeat at the hands of the ebullient master, Walter Hagen.

Again Sarazen tells of having stomach cramps and nerves that night—"as if every tie in the tracks had a point on it"—and he admits to getting no more than three or four hours of sleep. And, worse yet, when they arrived at New York's Grand Central Station the next morning, it was raining hard, and had been for a few days. The course was soggy and slow, hardly the ideal situation to make up a two-hole deficit in match play with the world's premier golfer.

And again, the Hagen flair for flamboyance showed itself. Sarazen had received a note at the club that morning, attached to tie box. The note said: "You probably don't remember me, but I'm that blond you met from the Follies. Don't look for me in the gallery. I don't want to take your mind off Hagen. But wear this tie for good luck." It was a horrendous orange-and-white tie, but not wishing to offend, Sarazen wore it, and by noon of the match, with the rain intermittently heavy, all the orange had washed off.

But he played well, and birdied the second hole, a 138-yard affair after putting a mashie shot ten inches from the cup. Hagen came back and retaliated with a birdie four on the long third, to go two up again.

Now, however, Sarazen's nerves had calmed and his cramps

had been placated, and he began playing Sarazen golf. Which is to say, outstanding golf. He evened the match by parring the fourth and getting a birdie on the fifth, and finally took his first lead by winning the eighth and ninth. Haig rallied, winning three holes on the back nine with birdies, but Sarazen birdied twice and took a one-stroke lead to lunch.

They sat together, and while partaking of a hearty meal, Hagen looked up and said: "Say, kid, that's quite a tie. Where'd you get it?"

"From a friend," Sarazen replied, picking at his food but not in the mood for either small talk or repast.

"Just a friend, gave you such a handsome tie?" Hagen said in mock outrage. "Why, I thought I had written in that note that your mysterious admirer was a Follies girl who wanted you to pay strict attention to beating Hagen."

But there was a more serious assignment at hand: maintaining the stroke lead over the great Hagen, who was acting as though he were ten strokes in front with nine holes left to play.

After 63 holes Sarazen was two up, but Hagen, who had made several rather miraculous charges in the past year, was not ready to be dismissed. Sarazen, playing as a man possessed, maintained the pressure. He shot the last seven holes brilliantly, canning an eagle-three on the 65th and holing out on the 70th, the putt he needed to put the match away, 3 and 2. The Haig had been beaten by the twenty-year-old boy, and he was the first to offer sincere congratulations. But he could not resist a final dig.

"You played great golf, kid," he said. "You had to, to beat Walter Hagen."

And four hours after the thrilling victory, Gene Sarazen was on an operating table in St. Luke's Riverside Hospital in Yonkers, New York—undergoing an emergency appendectomy.

The stomach pains and the cramps had not been nerves

after all. Truly, it had been a courageous day. And an electric one for the fanciers of golf in the United States.

Walter Hagen was born in 1893, the son of an East Rochester, New York, blacksmith. Francis Ouimet was born the same year, and so both were twenty when Ouimet won his "shot heard 'round the world" U.S. Open championship at Brookline.

But the greatest of maybes in that tournament, the most intriguing of "might have beens" occurred when The Haig skyrocketed to a final-round, fourteenth hole score of seven, three over par. For, by the kid's own gaudy admission, "If I could have saved three shots there, I would have made it a four-way tie. Then I would probably have won it all the next day."

But he did take the seven and he could not change it. The result was enough to list him in the official finish as tied for second place with Americans Jim Barnes and MacDonald Smith and France's Louis Tellier, a credible enough feat for a wet-behind-the-ears lad of twenty. But the unplayable lie of that fourteenth—a drive which had buried itself in a bunker wall and required two slaps to dislodge—upset and annoyed the brash youngster. "I'll be back," he promised, "and when I am, they'll spell my name right, too." He was referring to the account of the tournament in a Boston newspaper, which had erroneously named the young American as one W.C. Hagin.

He had promised to return, and he did. The next year he beat an elite field of the best professionals and amateurs in the world and won the 1914 U.S. Open, this time at Skokie, Illinois.

The Haig had already made himself known to the older, more staid golfers of the time. He had paraded up to Johnny McDermott, the defending champion, prior to the start of play in 1913 while they were dressing in the locker room.

"Aren't you Johnny McDermott, the champ?" he asked

boldly. "Hi. I'm W.C. Hagen from Rochester and I've come
to help you boys take care of Vardon and Ray."

McDermott stared at this youngster, done up in a striped
silk shirt, white flannel trousers, white buckskin shoes with red
rubber soles, and a red bandana around his neck as the finishing flourish, then barely gasped out a condescending greeting.

No one was flashier than Hagen. No one was more loudly
dressed for matches. But he had a reason, and he once tried to
explain why he outfitted himself in this fantastic collection of
outrageous colors.

"That was done to get my opponent's eyes and mind off
the ball," he said. "When the boys saw me it reminded them
of a sunset, plus some additional pastels. It used to make them
a bit dizzy. And of course, when they were dizzy, I took a
hole or two now and then. Sometimes I'd win a title."

There was, however, a serious side to Hagen's golf. He
prided himself on total, one hundred per cent concentration.

"If you can concentrate on your game, on each shot you
make, and make each shot with the intensity of a man who
will die rather than fail, you can be champion at any age.
Twenty, thirty, forty or fifty, it doesn't matter. But when a
man passes into his thirties, he has so many other interests in
life that he concentrates on golf progress only spasmodically.
The boy has but one interest. That is to win. He shoots the
works on every shot."

Perhaps there, in the midst of a serious moment, Hagen
summed up his fabulous career. Shoot the works. Take the
chance and unnerve the opponent. Find the edge, wherever
and whatever it may be, and capitalize on it.

He often worked an unsettling gambit on his opponents
even before the match began. "Well," he'd say, rolling his
eyes heaven-ward and putting just the right tone of boredom
into his voice, "who's going to be second in this tournament?"

He appreciated a story once told about the brilliant lawyer, Clarence Darrow, who, to capture the attention of a

jury while the prosecuting attorney was summing up, lit a specially-prepared long cigar. He had run a thin wire through it, and the jurors found themselves hypnotized by the growing length of the ash. It would not fall, and Darrow made sure to smoke it in a most pretentious fashion.

Hagen put this ploy to work in the final of the PGA championship of 1926, played that year on the Salisbury, Long Island, course. His foe was Leo Diegel, a top golfer of the day, and The Haig began conceding four- and five-foot putts early in the match. Diegel, astounded but no fool, would quickly pick up and thank Hagen for his noblesse oblige.

But Walter had a method to his apparent madness. Late in the match, when the pressure intensified, when each shot was taken with the care of a diamond-cutter, Diegel chipped up to within twenty-two inches of the cup. The figure is exact, because Hagen's caddy went back later to measure. Diegel looked up, expecting another concession, but Hagen said nothing. He stared at Diegel for what seemed like a full moment. Then he turned his back. Diegel became uneasy, uncertain. He was suspicious.

"There must be a roll here I don't know about," he said to his caddy. And with hands shaking, he putted—and missed.

Hagen went on to an easy 5 and 3 victory.

His 1914 Open victory, in which he played confident of success from the onset, was earned by a single stroke over a young amateur named Chick Evans. Hagen shot a brilliant 68 in the first round, but then blew up and scored middle rounds of 74 and 75 before coming in with a 73 to clinch the championship. After that, he went into a puzzling slump—a sudden loss of concentration, as he termed it, that would not cease until five years later, when he won his second Open at Brae Burn.

Perhaps his most phenomenal golf was played in the PGA tournaments of 1924, 1925, 1926, and 1927, when he won an unprecedented four consecutive titles. The PGA was conducted on a match-play basis then, and Hagen won twenty-two straight matches, a tournament record. He finally lost to Leo Diegel in the 1928 PGA held in Baltimore. Overall, he won forty individual PGA matches.

A somewhat premature retirement was suddenly announced in 1940, when Hagen, perhaps an ultimate victim of his high-living days, lost the sharp-focused skills that had propelled him to the top of the golf world.

"I just cannot bear the thought of firing an eighty," he said. "So I just won't take the chance. I have retired."

Sarazen played longer than did Hagen, and in his latter years he was, for extended periods, as gifted as he was years before. Many have called him the throwback, for he played golf when the tournaments were new and unpopular and hardly recognized, and he played the tour—the money trail—when golf was in the midst of its incredible Midas boom. He had played with Bobby Jones and Hagen; with Sam Snead and Ben Hogan; Ralph Guldahl and Chick Evans; and Jack Nicklaus and Arnold Palmer.

And Gene Sarazen remained a doer, an activist, in his sport. He lobbied for shorter courses, larger cups, faster playing. He argued that putting had become "half the score" in the sport because of the smallness of the holes. He argued also that the game had become, in the 1950's and 1960's, a game for the power hitters. "They are building the courses too long," he insisted. "Little people cannot compete with the big drivers."

Many of his proposals were greeted with little more than tolerant silence, but Sarazen, perhaps expecting that, continued his harangues. After all, he had been one of the best—at times, the absolute best—and he deserved to be heard.

Perhaps no better golf was ever played, for example, than the rounds he put together in the 1932 U.S. Open at Fresh Meadow in Long Island. With twenty-eight holes to play, Sarazen was eight strokes behind the leaders, Bobby Cruickshank and T. Phillip Perkins. Then he unleashed what Bobby

Jones later called "the finest competitive exhibition on record." He blazed away the final twenty-eight in a score of 100, and made his victory an almost one-sided one—three strokes ahead at the end with 286.

On that final round, Perkins fired a 70 and Cruickshank 68, to finish in a deadlock at 289. Sarazen, who had started much later, was, of course, aware of his situation. He had to attack, play boldly and devil take the hindmost. He went out in 4-5-3 2-5-3 4-4-2 for a front-nine of 32. And he came back in with a second-nine card that read 4-4-3 4-3-3 5-4-4, good for a 34 and an eighteen-hole total of 66, at that time the lowest round ever shot in the Open.

Sarazen basked in the glory of that one, made the most of his victory and continued to roll in the cash. But he did so deservingly, for he had by then acquired a reputation for the unexpected—indeed, the impossible—and no tournament demonstrates that more forcibly than the Masters of 1935. He was out of it when he came to the fifteenth hole of the final round, needing three birdies on the last four holes at Augusta, Georgia, to tie Craig Wood for the lead. Wood was already in the clubhouse with a 282 total.

And then, of course, came the miraculous Double Eagle. Capital letters are indicated here because there had never been a shot like it before in major competitive golf and there are legions of players who say nothing like it has been achieved since.

The fifteenth hole at Augusta is a par-5, 485-yard straightaway with a pond and several sand traps as none-too-friendly companions.

But let Sarazen tell it, as he has so often in the years since:

"My drive on the fifteenth had been exceptionally long, as I had a tail-end hook on it and the ground was hard. I was paired with Hagen in that final day, and as we walked after our drives, I heard a roar. Word soon came back to us that Wood had birdied for a three on the last hole, and was in with 282. When we reached our balls, I looked and asked my caddy, Stovepipe, what I needed to win. He looked surprised, and Haig was giggling. 'Boss,' he said, 'you need four threes.'

"Well, I figured if things were all that bad, I might as well go for broke."

And so Gene Sarazen decided to use a four-wood. He was 235 yards away and he eschewed a three-wood because of the lie of the ball, deep in the grass. He hit hard, and the ball rose in a low, buzzing trajectory, never rising more than twenty-five to thirty-five feet off the ground. It headed for the green, lofting easily over the pond. It kept going, on and on and on, and then it bounded. It landed on the green, bounced true, still running in a straight line, and then the gallery behind the green erupted in a cacophony of noise.

"I knew then that the ball had gone into the hole," Sarazen said. "I couldn't believe it, and sometimes I still don't, but I knew it had gone in. I had made a double-eagle two."

That shot gave him all the edge he needed. He parred the the sixteenth (after missing a ten-foot birdie putt that stopped inches short) and settled for another par-four on seventeen. On eighteen he hit a fair-to-middling drive and then slammed another four-wood to the green. The shot landed four feet past the pin, but rolled disastrously another thirty feet up a slope. Now it was down to last chances. Holing out would mean the tournament championship outright, two-putting would earn him a tie and force a playoff, three-putting would end the magnificent finish.

He hit the ball and it died three feet shy of the cup. Saying later that "too much analysis would have been a bad thing in that spot," Sarazen simply strode after the ball and, as it had barely stopped rolling, slapped it home. He had tied Craig Wood.

Of course, he won the 36-hole playoff with little effort. He shot 36, 35, 36, and 37 for a 144 and Wood was five strokes off at 149—four back after the first eighteen.

The Double-Eagle had worked its magic on Craig Wood, too. He did not stop talking about it, and it most certainly "psyched him out" in the playoff. Sarazen had become a destined winner, and Wood sensed it.

The Masters of 1935 was Sarazen's last major tournament triumph, although he remained competitive for thirty years more. He always felt the secret of golf was in the swing, and agreed with his peer and rival, Hagen, that winning golf is not for the young man exclusively.

"Hit the ball well, hit it consistently well, and you can play for years. Physical strength is not necessarily the thing, although today it seems to help. The swing is everything. If his swing is basically proper, fundamentally correct, a golfer can continue to play well for a long, long time."

For Gene Sarazen, it worked, for he did play well many years after others of his time found golf had suddenly fled and all that remained were memories.

Walter Hagen? He died on October 5, 1969, mourned by millions who had come to love his style, his regal demeanor, his laughter. Sarazen was one of those who openly wept at his death.

They were paired, those two, in much more than a game. They had become integral parts of each other's legends, and as such they will always be part of the greater legend that has become golf. Their game.

CHAPTER THREE

Bobby Jones Wins Golf's Grand Slam — 1930

IF ONE WERE TO CHOOSE A SINGLE YEAR AS THE MOST dramatic in the history of golf, it would be 1930. And if one had to select a single event as the most outstanding in the history of this sport (assuming one had the gracious permission to consider a prestigious multiple feat one event) it would be Bobby Jones' Grand Slam of that year.

Bobby Jones is regarded by most experts as the foremost amateur player in history and one of the three most gifted golfers this world has seen, amateur or professional. The name itself serves to identify the sport, and there are precious few superstars who are capable of overreaching even their own lofty status to dwarf a sport. But Bobby Jones is one of those few. He is still known today, not for all the particulars and details of a wondrous but strangely short career, but for the one crowning achievement—the Grand Slam—when he held the world of golf in stunned respect.

Bobby Jones, in that magic year, won the U.S. Amateur and Open Championships and the British Amateur and Open Championships. It was unprecedented and unimaginable. It was Babe Ruth and his sixty home runs of 1927. It was Gertrude Ederle swimming the English Channel. It was Charles Lindbergh flying the Atlantic; Thomas Alva Edison speaking the first words into the mouthpiece of a machine he named "telephone."

Bobby Jones was an Atlanta, Georgia, boy who first discovered the game of golf by following his parents around the East Lake Country Club course when he was five, and it was this boy who later told his father: "I like fishing and baseball better. Golf's too slow."

But he had been bitten. He had uncovered the joy of a solidly hit drive, the thrill of a perfectly lofted chip shot, the exhilaration of a putt surely winding its way across a green to thump into the cup. He was eleven years old when Francis Ouimet won the U.S. Open in 1913; he was twenty-eight when he became golf's next super performer.

Even before that happened, he had become as dominant a sports personage as the other giants of his era: Bill Tilden, Jack Dempsey, Earl Sande, Babe Ruth. He became folklore before he was twenty-five, the original Jones Boy.

Bobby Jones was a rarity. He was the perfect (if you will, the complete) golfer; he was the precision driver, the flawless putter, the relentless pursuer of his own private and personal devil—perfection. He did what he set out to do in the face of unprecedented odds, in the face of history, and with the knowledge that every superb golfer before him had failed in this particular crusade.

He had claimed nine major championships before 1930, nine that would have assured his place in golf's Hall of Fame long before the Grand Slam. He started with his first U.S. Open championship in 1923. That was followed by the U.S. Amateur title in 1924 and again in 1925; the U.S. and British Opens in 1926; the U.S. Amateur and British Open in 1927; the U.S. Amateur again in 1928, and the U.S. Open in 1929. Five times, both before and after the Slam, he was a member of the United States' Walker Cup team, and his record stands as five matches played, five matches won.

Then came 1930.

Step One was the British Amateur on the hoary St. Andrews links in Scotland. He scrambled and scratched his way through the early matches but finally gained the final and absolutely drowned his competition, one Roger Wethered,

7 and 6. The crowd of 25,000, completely taken with this man-child from the colonies, honored him with a spirit and abandon not typical of stoic British behavior.

He had won it, and he needed a moving armada of police and course officials to get him through the galleries to the clubhouse. There, a weary but emotionally delirious young man paid tribute to the tradition of which he had become a part:

"I would rather have won this tournament," he said, "than any other in the world."

The next step was the British Open at Hoylake. It was, perhaps, the least brilliant of the four victories, for, although he started out well—firing off rounds of 70 and 72 in the first two days—he faltered badly and closed with scores of 74 and 75 for a total of 291. And he finished early, thus being forced to chew his fingernails until two other Americans, Macdonald Smith and Leo Diegel, were through with their frantic charges at the leader's score. But they both fell short, coming in at 293, and the championship belonged to the Jones Boy, the amateur from Atlanta.

He returned to America as a conquering hero, but already the possibility of a never-before-accomplished Grand Slam was the topic of the sports pages from coast to coast. Could he do it? Would he lose his nerve, his will, his courage?

They waited to find out, waited until the best in the game met at Minneapolis Interlochen golf course for the U.S. Open.

It was the thirty-fourth Open tournament in American history, but it had by far the greatest following and appeal to golfers and the public. They key competition was expected to come from two men named Smith—Macdonald and Horton. Also included in the star-studded field were such top-flight competitors as Harry Cooper, Tommy Armour, John Golden, Johnny Farrell, Craig Wood, Leo Diegel, and Charley Lacey. Each of them was capable of winning handily. It was, indeed, a meeting of champions, a tourney to test the mettle of this lad.

Despite a laudable 71, Jones found himself one stroke behind Macdonald Smith and Tommy Armour at the end of the first round. And he was a trifle farther back after the second round when he fired a 73 and watched Horton Smith put a 70 after a 72, and saw Harry Cooper tie him with a pair of 72's. They called him Lighthorse Harry Cooper and he, too, was famed for charges, for his ability to snatch a victory in the last, desperate moments of a tournament.

Jones was favored now, but sentimentally. Too many guns were stacked against him on the other side of the road.

And then Jones tore them up. He chewed up their tradition and their odds and their sympathy and he spit them back with a startling 68 on the third round. He finished that round five strokes ahead of the rest, after Mac Smith had skyrocketed to a 74, Lighthorse Harry to a 73, Horton Smith to a 76, and Tommy Armour to a 75. Only one other man was to play a round in the 1930 Open in the sixties, and he was a forgotten pro from Virginia, California, named Monte Dutra, who sandwiched a third-round 69 around scores of 76, 78, and 80.

The final day was an anticlimax. Bobby tried hard to be serious, to maintain his iron calm, but the big lead and the lack of competition from a field that should have provided a solid challenge seduced him into relaxing. He came in with 75, finished with 287 and still beat Mac Smith—who charged back with a final round 70—by two strokes.

And then there was Merion, the suburban golf course in the gentle foothills outside Philadelphia, the site of the thirty-fourth U.S. Amateur Championship, September 22nd through September 27th, inclusive.

Was he nervous? No, only the fantastically swelled gallery and his opponents were. Was he awed by the great scope of his ambitions? Not a chance. He was Bobby Jones, he had golf by its tail, and he was swinging from the heels.

The first round opponent in this match-play classic was a Canadian named Ross Somerville. No chance, Ross. The score was 5 and 4. That same afternoon, he took on another Canadian, Fred Hoblitzel, and the score was the same, another resounding 5 and 4 triumph.

But if those two matches appeared easy, the rest were cake. He destroyed Fay Coleman of the California Country Club, 6 and 5, and then totally swamped his former Walker Cup teammate, Jess Sweetser, 9 and 8, to gain the final round. He was 36 holes from immortality, and he never wavered.

It was as if every shot was computer-chosen and precision-ordered. He had evolved, long before, the perfect swing a Scot writer described as "standing over the ball casually, as if engaged in ordinary conversation . . . a swing of beauty . . . of all the millions of golfers in the world, I do not suppose there is another who swings a club back so smoothly or so sweetly."

His opponent was Gene Homans, a seasoned veteran from the Englewood (New Jersey) Country Club, and poor Eugene never had a chance. The final score was 8 and 7, and Bobby Jones had achieved the first and only Grand Slam in history, the championships of the two major American and British Open and Amateur tournaments.

Two months later, Bobby Jones, at the age of 28, announced his retirement. One is left to speculate on what might have occurred had he stayed with it, had he turned professional. The millions of dollars that were waiting to be won could have all been marked with his initials, for he was at the peak of his game. No one could have touched him. But he left the competitive tour to make instructional movies, and soon afterward moved into the commander's seat of the administration of the venerable Masters Tournament, a position he occupies to this day.

Bobby Jones had made history, and he was content to let history make the most of Bobby Jones.

There is, perhaps, another area to explore in the study of Bobby Jones. We have, of course, paid tribute to his Grand Slam, and to the precision of his golf, the method by which he elevated a game to a science. We have enumerated his triumphs and lauded his championships, and well we should, for it has already been stated that perhaps no other man ever did more with a weighted stick and a little white ball.

To some individuals, perhaps, words such as honor and principle and sportsmanship have lost their ring. They have grown tainted by overuse or have been cheapened by abuse. It is quite possible that today a man such as Bobby Jones would not attract the reverence or extract the affection of a nation as he did four decades ago. One hopes this is not so, that there will always be a place for such men.

The late and famed sportswriter, Grantland Rice, was an unabashed fan of Bobby's. In 1940, he wrote: "There is no more chance that golf will give the world another Jones than there is that literature will produce another Shakespeare, sculpture another Phidias, music another Chopin. There is no more probability that the next five hundred years will produce another Bob than there is that two human beings will be found with identical fingerprints."

Others, those who mattered in Bobby Jones' world, also submitted their respects to the pages of history:

"He was," declared Francis Ouimet, "absolutely perfect. It was discouraging and monotonous the way he hit practically every shot exactly as it should be hit. If he had come along fifteen or twenty years later, he still would have been the best."

Walter Hagen tried to capture the mystique that was Bobby Jones, too, and he did it succinctly, as was his style. "If I were asked to vote for the greatest golfer of all time," he said later in his life, "I'd have to mark my ballot for Bobby Jones."

To all he remained the gentleman, playing golf for fun and satisfaction, not for profit or cash benefits. He championed the amateur golfer more than anyone had done before and far more than anyone has done since. He maintained his amateur standing despite the easy pickings to be found on the burgeoning pro circuit, despite the manufacturers and sporting goods houses that were willing to pay fancy prices for his endorsements.

From that day when he told his father he much preferred "fishing and baseball," Bobby nevertheless built up his love for golf during his teens. By the time he was fourteen, he was ready. He had won several Atlanta and Georgia state amateur titles, and had taken the measure of some of the finer Southern amateur players. But he was, after all, merely a boy, hardly ready, they said, for what he decided to do.

What was it? He went to Philadelphia's Merion Cricket Club, to contest for the famed U.S. Amateur championship of 1916. The top players of the day were there, waiting for the unknown boy. There were Chick Evans and Robert Gardner, Jesse Guilford and G. P. Tiffany, Gardner White and John Anderson. And Bobby Jones.

He was matched with E. M. Byers in the first round, after having startled the entrants by leading the field with a 74 in the qualifier. Bobby Jones took on Byers and beat him, 3 and 1. Then they matched him with F. W. Dyer, another respected amateur, and he won this second round match, 4 and 2. Suddenly the crowd had become electrified, but it was all too much, too soon.

He was ousted in the semifinal round by defending champion Gardner White, who ultimately lost the championship to Chick Evans, 4 and 3. But they all remembered the slim Southerner, the boy who had almost tamed the men in early September of 1916. The country's involvement in World War I forced the cancellation of the Amateur championship in 1917 and 1918, but when it was resumed in 1919, there was Bobby Jones, firing away at Oakmont in Pittsburgh. He qualified easily with a 159, second best of the field of 150 entries, and defeated J. B. Manion in the first round of match play, 3 and 2. Next Gardner White fell, in an act of retribution, 5 and 4. Then it was R. E. Knepper who felt the sting of the seventeen-year-old's swing and was eliminated, 3 and 2.

After that it was W. C. Fownes, of the home course, who met young Bobby Jones in the semifinal round. And Fownes fell before the onslaught of the machine-like swing, the power of the thinking man's (boy's?) golfer, 5 and 3. For the championship, it was S. D. Herron, also of Oakmont—and now the famed "championship jinx" that plagued Bobby Jones made its first appearance. He was soundly defeated, 5 and 4.

But 1920 saw him reach the semifinal before losing to Francis Ouimet, 6 and 5. And in 1921, after fashioning incredible victories of 12 and 11 against Clarence Wolff and 9 and 8 over Dr. O. F. Willing, Bobby lost to William I. Hunter, an Englishman, 2 and 1. A semifinal round loss to Jess Sweetser in 1922, at The Country Club, and a defeat in the third round to Max Marston in 1923 at Flossmoor, Illinois, preceded his first Amateur championship, in 1924.

That victory bears repeating, for although he had won the U.S. Open in 1923, the year before, he always regarded the Amateur as the tournament he most wanted to win, because he was, after all, the scion of the country's amateurs.

He had qualified beautifully in the 1924 Amateur, again held at the Merion Cricket Club, with a 144, second only (by two strokes) to D. Clark Cockran. He met W. J. Thompson of Canada in the first round and swept to a 6 and 5 victory. Cockran fell next, 3 and 2. In the semifinal round, he again slapped past Knepper with near disdain, 6 and 4, and then literally destroyed the proud Ouimet in the next round, 11 and 10.

At last he had reached the final. His opponent was the

revered George Von Elm, but Von Elm was not about to match Bobby Jones that 27th of September. When the dust had settled, Von Elm fully realized the devastation that had been visited on his golfing reputation, the score was 9 and 8 —nine holes up with eight to play. And so the world of amateur golf had a new champion.

Bobby won it again in 1925, defending the championship in the final round against Watts Gunn, a fellow Atlantan, 8 and 7. In 1926, Von Elm gained some sort of revenge by wresting the title from Bobby in the final match, 2 and 1, but in 1927 the crown shifted back to Mr. Jones, who ran roughshod over Chick Evans for the championship, 8 and 7. And what of 1928? Why, it was Mr. Jones again, defeating Thomas P. Perkins of Great Britain, on the Pebble Beach, California, course, by the ludicrous score of 10 and 9.

He was, truly, the finest amateur golfer of his time.

Jones often remarked that some of his most satisfying times on a golf course occurred during Walker Cup competition. He played on five Walker Cup teams—1922, 1924, 1926, 1928 and 1930—and never lost a singles match. His victories were achieved to the admiration and cheers of a British gallery, after the Americans had already sold him their hearts and souls.

In 1922, playing at the Southampton, New York, National Links course, Bobby teamed with Jess Sweetser for a 3 and 2 doubles win, and then triumphed over Roger H. Wethered, again by a 3 and 2 score, in his individual match. In 1924, at the Garden City (New York) Golf Club, Bobby teamed with William Fownes for the first and only defeat of any kind he tasted in this competition, a 1-up victory by Michael Scott and Robert Scott, Jr. But he easily triumphed in his singles competition, 4 and 3, over Major Charles O. Hezlet.

In 1926, at the fabled St. Andrews course in Scotland, Bobby and Watts Gunn—the Atlanta tandem—beat Cyril

Tolley and Andrew Jamieson, Jr., 4 and 3, after which Bobby scored the second most one-sided singles decision of the Walker Cup series, swamping Tolley, 12 and 11.

The most one-sided victory? That occurred the next year, when Bobby beat T. Philip Perkins, 13 and 12, after teaming with Chick Evans to pound out a 5 and 3 decision in the doubles match.

Finally, in the glory year of 1930, Bobby closed out his Walker Cup competition with an awesome 9 and 8 victory over Wethered. He also teamed with Dr. Willing to score an 8 and 7 doubles triumph at the Royal St. George's Golf Club in Sandwich, England.

In recounting the glittering career of Bobby Jones, one must wonder about the single round he considered the best he ever played. Unlike so many other sports heroes, who immodestly begin to recount several great moments, Bobby Jones points directly to his qualifying round for the 1926 British Open.

Playing on a course known for its long fairways, rolling greens, and gigantic sand traps and water hazards—the Sunningdale Golf Club—Bobby shot 66, which was six under par. It was here that he displayed his completely flawless swing and his intellectual approach to the game, for every shot was hit in a perfectly coordinated fashion. He played each hole as if housing a calculator in his head. His card shows not a 5 and not a 2, as he rattled off a front nine of 4-4-4 3-3-4 4-3-4 and a back nine of 4-3-4 3-4-3 4-4-4. After such a start, the Open itself proved to be child's play, and Bobby won it easily with a score of 291. Hagen and Von Elm finished in a tie for third behind Al Watrous.

A ticker-tape parade down New York's famed Broadway was in store for the Atlantan soon after he annexed the U.S. Open with a 293, despite a near-disastrous 79 on the second round. This time, however, Grand Slam glory was not in store for him, since he lost the U.S. Amateur to George Von Elm, 2 and 1, in the final played at Baltusrol Country Club in Springfield, New Jersey.

That loss, incidentally, is more than noteworthy. It marked the last time Jones was to lose a 36-hole match in major competition for the remainder of his career.

Indeed, Von Elm's victory prevented Jones from closing out the final seven years—count them, seven—of his incredible career undefeated.

In today's realm of cold-blooded competition, where thousands of dollars ride on each swing, each putt, the charm and graciousness practiced by Bobby Jones has become a mourned victim. He was, as has been stated before, the epitome of sportsmanship. And he inspired the same behavior from those he played against for championships.

Perhaps, to fully appreciate the mood of the man in this respect, one can go back to his loss to George Von Elm at Baltusrol, the last major tournament to escape him.

It was, of course, a match for a championship, and the pressure was at a high pitch. After all, winning the U.S. Amateur, then as now, was a prestigious accomplishment and the fact that Bobby had won it before and was to win it again was immaterial.

Von Elm, too, had established a reputation as a killer in match play; he was an emotionless man whose kindness stopped after a cursory "hello" on the first tee. Silent and disciplined, he remained intent on the game and bent on pressuring his opponents with a careful avoidance of any outward show of friendliness.

But it was not possible to play that way with Bobby Jones. A revealing incident in this tournament bears this out.

At the seventeenth green of the morning round, both chipped on the green and lined up their putting approaches. Von Elm was "away" and so he had the first putt. And he hit a dandy, from approximately fifteen feet to within a foot of the cup. Then Bobby putted, overran his attempt at a birdie and sank it coming back for the par five.

With that, the Jones-inspired gallery let loose a cheer and began heading for the eighteenth, leaving Von Elm standing over his short putt, puzzled by the sudden departure of the crowd and curious as to whether he was going to lose Bobby, too, before he holed out.

But Bobby, sensing his discomfort, strode up to the ball and tapped it back to Von Elm. The crowd froze, hushed, not at all expecting something as rare as this.

"You go ahead, George," he said. "I'll give you that one."

Von Elm was astounded at the gesture, and on the very next green he reciprocated, giving Jones a putt of about thirty inches. In a match of such meaning, a contest of such competitive pressure, these two—at Bobby's instigation—proved again that amateurs are good sports. Both were warmly applauded for their actions, and Jones, who lost the match in the afternoon, was equally gracious in the presentation of the tournament's championship.

"You cannot expect any golfer to go on beating a player as talented as Von Elm," he said. "It was my privilege to stay close to him."

Then, in November of 1930, after accomplishing all there was to strive for in golf, Bobby Jones announced his retirement. Perhaps the fact of the Grand Slam had some effect on his decision, for the impact of what he had done caused him to question what would be left to shoot for in the years ahead. He once admitted to a friend, his constant companion O.B. Keeler, that he feared further competitive golf would prove to be "anti-climactic."

Also, he pointed to the increasing pressure as another factor in his ultimate decision. "It just isn't fun any longer," he said. "In the beginning, nothing much was expected of me, and I enjoyed battling the older fellows. I enjoyed the challenge of beating, or attempting to beat, the top players of the day.

"But as I began winning more and more, and as more and more was expected of me, I found the pressure distasteful. It was no longer fun, and I had always played golf for the fun of it. When it got to be 1925 or so, and when golf became a serious business for me, I was expected to win or finish well up in every tournament I entered. After the big year (1930), I decided I had had enough. I chose the easier and more gracious life of non-competitive golf."

It is the same type of reasoning that led to the retirements of such immortal sporting figures as the late Rocky Marciano, Joe DiMaggio, and Jimmy Brown. They had achieved so much that to continue meant only a certain downhill slide. And in their champions' hearts, the far brighter alternative was to step out at the peak of their careers, still respected and remembered for the greatness of their accomplishments, hesitant to grow older and less precise in their sport in full view of a national audience.

Bobby Jones retired, and all men pointed to his Grand Slam as the top achievement. But some have stated that winning the four tournaments in 1930 was not the big moment. In the last nine years of his tournament activity, from 1922 through 1930, he participated in a dozen national open championships, both in the United States (nine) and Britain (three). And in those dozen attempts, he either won or finished second eleven times. It is a monument to consistent brilliance, and this author, for one, ranks that record as the finest tribute to Bobby Jones.

His decision to abandon the golf circuit was greeted with universal melancholia, for to lose a golfer of his charisma and brilliance was to lose an idol, a hero. *The New York Times* summed it up neatly: "With dignity he quit the memorable scene on which he nothing common did, or mean."

CHAPTER FOUR

Ben Hogan Wins Masters, U.S. Open, and British Open — 1953

THE CAREENING TERROR OF AN AUTOMOBILE GONE OUT of control on a highway is more vivid than a nightmare, for it is a nightmare of the conscious. If fortunate enough to live through such horror, one can never forget the unnerving brush with death at high speed, the sickening crash of metal on metal, the skidding and spinning to disaster.

In 1949, on the second day of February, Ben Hogan was in such an accident, on a lonely Texas highway near the tiny town of Van Horn. He was nearly killed. With him in the car, on a trip from Phoenix, Arizona to his home in Fort Worth, was his wife, Valerie, whom he saved from certain injury and possible death by flinging himself across her body seconds before the car smashed into a speeding bus which had suddenly cut across the highway from an access road.

The screech of brakes and the awful realization that nothing could stop the crash burned itself into Ben Hogan's memory, but the miraculous recovery he fought to make has burned with equal intensity into the minds of sports fans everywhere.

This, then, is more than a story about a golfer. It is a tale of bravery and courage, dedication and determination, and a proud will that fought against what appeared inevitable. It is much more than the recounting of a championship golfer's finest moments and brilliant years. It is, rather, a guidepost from which others can take their share of satisfaction and joy through Ben Hogan's successful battle with adversity.

Before that fateful day in 1949, Ben Hogan had already established himself as one of the finest shot-makers in the history of the game. His many honors included the 1948 U.S. Open championship, the 1946 and 1948 PGA laurels, a then-record 276 score in the U.S. Open of 1948, the Vardon Trophy of 1940, 1941, and 1948, a runner-up berth in the 1946 Masters, and membership on the 1947 Ryder Cup team.

And then came the tragedy.

Ben had been returning from Phoenix, where he and his one close friend, Jimmy Demaret, had tied for the tournament lead, forcing a playoff. And Ben, for once not able to beat his friendly rival, settled for second place. After the playoff, Ben decided to pass up the next stop on the tour—the Tucson Open—and go home with Valerie, to a house they had purchased a scant eight days before.

So they left Phoenix and Demaret and other friends, and began the trek home in their new car which had been purchased from golf winnings. And then, on U.S. Highway 80, their world almost came to an end.

After the crash, which ultimately involved five vehicles in a foggy fugue of tragedy, spectators on the scene assumed Hogan was dead. He lay motionless, his head on Val's lap. When the doctors finally arrived, they covered his body—and his face. But Val heard a barely-audible groan, and she whipped off the blanket in a frenzy of hope. And he was alive —just barely alive.

The hospital in El Paso was called the Hotel Dieu, the Hotel of God, and never was a name more aptly given. It was four hours before the confusion was resolved out there on the highway, four full hours before someone had thought to summon aid, four hours before Ben Hogan began receiving the vitally needed medical assistance.

He had suffered a broken collarbone, a double fracture of the pelvis, a fractured left ankle, smashed and splintered ribs, and several internal injuries.

It was two days—days of intensive care and prayer—before the medical team assigned to him could even risk moving him.

Even when the first early crises had safely passed, the doctors were not very sanguine about the future.

"There is legitimate reason to fear that Ben Hogan will never walk again," said one of the doctors. "I would not even care to speculate on his chances to play golf ever again. He is lucky to simply be alive." But they were not aware of Ben Hogan's will, of his tremendous drive.

Slowly he began to heal, to come back from near tragedy. And all that time Val sat at his bedside, erect and proud and not willing to crumble into tears, because she, more than anyone, knew how tough Ben really was inside. If it could be beaten, she later told a friend, Ben would be the one to beat it.

He did. And then he almost didn't.

After it seemed he was going to upset every dire prediction, the blood clots began. Their invasion was fast and sinister. One moved up his damaged left leg and lodged itself in a lung. A week later, another did the same. He dropped from his normal 142 pounds to a mere 118. There was fresh panic.

It then became apparent that surgery would be needed: a draining of the vena cava, the major artery in the lower body and upper legs. It would have to be tied off to prevent any further clot danger from the affected left leg.

This crisis was perhaps the most serious, for the doctors at the Hotel Dieu could not perform the operation. Instead, Dr. Alton S. Ochsner, a surgical professor at the Tulane Medical School in New Orleans, was recommended. Val called him, and he simply asked when it was necessary. Still another problem presented itself; there were no chartered airliners available on such short notice and, because of heavy rains and low altitude between New Orleans and Fort Worth, commercial service had been snarled.

Ben began to fade. He became delirious. He called for golf clubs and caddies, he recounted holes he had played, tournaments he had won. His brother, Royal, called the commanding officer of the Briggs Air Force Base in El Paso, General David W. Hutchinson, who was a friend of Ben's. By morning a B-29, carrying Dr. Ochsner, landed in El Paso.

He took one look at Ben and called for an operating room, and after acquiring Ben's consent (Val insisted on that) he began the touchy work. It was a success. The vena cava was tied off and circulation in his damaged left leg was slowed to the absolute minimum. But it was felt that by saving his life, Dr. Ochsner had killed off Ben's golf career.

Nevertheless, Ben lived, and he regained his health and vitality. He began holding a golf club in his hospital bed, swinging it over his head, perfecting the grip unique to Ben Hogan. He had assembled a series of exercise bars over his bed, and with his good arm (the collarbone had not yet knit) he began lifting himself. Rubber balls were on the bedstand for him to squeeze, to bring strength back to his hands.

He left Hotel Dieu twelve days later, boarded a train for Fort Worth, and began plotting the strategy for his comeback.

He began learning to walk again with the aid of a "walker," those rolling stands hospital patients are sometimes given. Three weeks later he discarded it, and began the painful ordeal of going solo. Up and down the stairs of his Fort Worth house he would go, time after time, day after day. He took to walking around the block, resting sometimes midway. Then he began to jog. He had beaten it, really beaten it. Now he had to answer the big question: would he ever play golf again?

That question began to be answered when he returned from England, where he had gone as the non-playing captain of the U.S. Ryder Cup team. He came home and began going to the Colonial Country Club in Fort Worth, hitting golf balls by the thousands.

And finally, he did come back. It was January of 1950, not

quite a year after the accident, and Ben had entered the Los Angeles Open. Could he do it? Could he still play golf? He shot a 68 in the practice round, and decided he was ready to resume competitive golf. He had asked the course announcer, Scotty Chisholm, to simply introduce him by name when he teed off on the first tee that opening day.

Scotty almost followed his directive. "This is the greatest event in the history of the Los Angeles Open," he said. "But I have been requested by Mr. Hogan to introduce him and say nothing else. On the tee is Ben Hogan."

He shot a 73 for the first round and followed it with a 69. Then he added another 69 in the third round and the same on the final day. He had put together a tournament score of 280, and he was in the lead.

But while he was in the locker room, Sam Snead came up with a fancy 66, sinking a twenty-foot putt on the eighteenth and forced a playoff. It was too much for Hogan's weary body. He went around in 76, and Snead won easily.

It had been done, however. Ben Hogan had come back.

The comeback continued in the years ahead, all leading up to what was going to be his finest hour, in 1953. That year he won the Masters, the U.S. Open, and the British Open—the Triple Sweep.

He was U.S. Open champion in 1951. He was Masters champion in 1951. He had won the U.S. Open in 1950, and since that was his first major triumph after the comeback, it bears retelling.

The time was June, the place the Merion Cricket Club outside of Philadelphia: a monstrous 6,696-yard, par-70 course famed and feared for its twisted fairways and greased-lightning greens. An incredibly difficult place from which to finish off a comeback.

On the first day, Ben shot a 72 while an unknown and unemployed pro from Alabama, Lee Mackey, Jr., shot a course record 64. But Mackey was no sudden sensation, no budding champion. He skyrocketed to an 81 for the second round and eventually finished in twenty-fifth place. Hogan came in the second day with a 69, which put him two strokes behind the leader, Dutch Harrison, going into the final 36 holes.

The third round was taut and tense as Hogan first caught Harrison with a 71 for 212, and then Lloyd Mangrum took the lead by one stroke at 211. In addition, Cary Middlecoff and Johnny Palmer caught Hogan and Harrison to create a four-way tie in second place, one stroke behind. The fourth round—the finisher for some, the glory-18 for one man—finally arrived. The man turned out to be Ben Hogan.

Middlecoff and Palmer faded and eliminated themselves with final rounds of 79. A Washington, D.C., pro named George Fazio stunned the gallery with a 70 and finished at 287, and as the day wore on that score began to look like a winner's total. Then Mangrum finished with a 76, enough to tie Fazio. Hogan reached the twelfth one over par. If he could play the final seven in as much as two over par, the tournament was his.

But he lost one stroke of his allotted two on twelve when he slapped an approach shot too strong and missed a five-foot putt coming back. He missed another short putt on fifteen for a bogey. Now he had to come in the rest of the way in no more than par. It was a test of champions.

He salvaged a scrambling par four on sixteen, a 445-yard devil. Seventeen was a long par three. Ben fell into a sand trap with his tee shot but pitched out to within five feet of the cup—only to miss yet another small putt. Now it was eighteen and no more chances. He needed a par on the 458-yard par-four to gain a tie. He was exhausted and his body ached, and the 8,000 frantic fans following his miracle kept the pressure high. He drove well, placed a two-iron shot pin high and forty feet away and rolled a putt within a yard of the cup. The second try was stroked in smoothly. He had tied Mangrum and Fazio, the sixth triple tie in what was then fifty Open championships.

The 18-hole playoff the next day was an anticlimax. Ben tore Merion into shreds, firing away for a 69 to Mangrum's 73 and Fazio's 75. He won the Open, the second of four such successes.

And now for his banner year—1953.

Hogan won the Masters by shooting rounds of 70-69-66-69, the 274 total setting a tournament record. He won the Open at Oakmont in Pittsburgh with 283, six strokes ahead of the runner-up, Sam Snead. Then he went to the British Open at Carnoustie. It was one of the few major tournaments that had eluded Ben Hogan up to this point. But there was a valid reason for this situation: he had never tried it before.

He won it easily, playing on a course made sodden by rain. He was given a ticker-tape parade down Broadway in New York, and upon being presented with the keys to the city on the steps of City Hall, he broke down. "You want to cry," he said haltingly. "I owe it to God and my wife, Valerie."

He also owed it to himself, to his courageous fight against odds and accident, sickness, and competition of the highest quality. It was, perhaps, his triumph at Carnoustie that cemented the man and the fable into one image forever bonded by time. He had to win the British Open to expand his reputation across the world, for in the golf-happy British Isles, no man is an international champion until he wins *their* Open.

All of America's top name golfers had won it before—the list included Walter Hagen, Bobby Jones, and Gene Sarazen—and it was only then that the proud English had given them their rightful share of honor. But Ben had never attempted to play in the British Open and this, too, had increased the desire on the part of the Britons that he should. He was implored to enter the tournament by such publications as Edinburgh's *Golf Monthly*, which, in an editorial, proclaimed:

Carnoustie, did he come and triumph, would impress the seal of Hogan's fame. In phantasy (sic) we see Hogan, the enigma, silent, austere, resolute, battling out of the wind-swept links of the Angus seaboard, one of the massive tests of the game in the world. Do not leave it too late, Ben, to take your place amongst the immortals and the supreme honour in the game. Scottish golfers, and especially Carnoustie, whose sons did so much for golf in your homeland, will take you to their hearts.

Ben finally accepted the challenge. He entered the British Open.

Ben took Val with him, and they flew to Carnoustie ten days before the tournament. And when he arrived he realized the trouble his body would have, for the weather was cold and damp, and the first indications of a back problem that to this day haunts the Hawk began to act as a drain on his stamina.

He was weak and debilitated. He lost weight and he came down with the flu. His temperature rose and his blood pressure dropped, and his wife candidly admitted she was "concerned" over his health. But he hit the course like a bomb, firing an honest 70 on the first round of the qualifying section of the tournament, which lasted for two days. He was the Hogan they all expected—silent, somber, solitary. But he was also the Hogan they expected to see on the course—a brilliant golfer.

The second round of the qualifying section turned to disaster. He toured in 75, had trouble sinking putts and gave the critics a picnic. A London newspaperman likened Hogan's golf to the kind "his grandmother might play."

Then they started shooting for real, and it was the Hogan everyone expected.

Frank Stranahan, a Toledo millionaire amateur, led after that first day with a 70, two under par. Roberto De Vicenzo had a 72, Hogan a 73, and Ben was absolutely livid because of the mistakes he had made. He came back the next morning and an observer said he never looked so serious and intent. He fired up the gallery by scoring six birdies on the first eight holes, but then lost his magic putting touch and came in with a 71. Still, it was a respectable round, and he trailed the two leaders—Britain's Dai Reese and Scotland's Eric Brown—by two strokes. They had totalled 142's; Ben had a 144.

They played the final 36 holes of the British Open on the last day, a Herculean chore for a well, sound man; an almost impossible task for a man in Hogan's condition. But early that morning, clad in two sweaters, he started his charge.

In the morning round, bolstered by iron shots that were fantastic in their accuracy and distance, Hogan shot a 70. That, too, would have been better but for a shaky putting performance. Yet that old battling spirit refused to flag. He fought back from successive bogeys on four and five with birdies on the sixth and seventh holes. Four more birdies on the back nine kept him in balance with two more bogeys, including a double-bogey six on seventeen. But he had his 70, and it was good enough to tie him with Di Vicenzo for the lead.

He ate his lunch right on the course, as he had done all during the tournament, and he smoked continually. But his nerves had held; the bad putting jitters of the morning round were not to appear again.

The afternoon 18 produced some of Hogan's finest golf. He did not three-putt a single green. Included in his bag of thrills that day was an incredible shot on the fifth hole. His second shot had slipped back into a bunker, fifty feet away from the cup. It was a difficult chip shot, much less an opportunity to hole out. But that is just what he did, knocking the ball into the cup and eliciting a tumultuous round of applause from the spectators.

John Derr, the longtime sportscaster for CBS Radio, was on the fairway at the fifteenth, sending home shot-by-shot accounts of Bantam Ben's finest hour. He recalls an exchange between himself and Hogan.

"Antonio Cerda, who was suddenly a challenger, was one away and playing the thirteenth. I told Ben of this, and he asked if Cerda was on the tee or the green. 'He's on the tee, Ben' I said, and Ben just looked away for a minute, thinking, puffing on a cigarette. Then Ben turned back to me and he said: 'Thanks, John. That'll be all.' I rate that one sentence my all-time sports thrill. When he said that sentence, I knew he was not going to lose."

No mistakes now, no disastrous holes, and the Open belonged to Ben Hogan. And Ben knew it. He played cautious, methodical golf designed to shoot par and come home a winner. He parred fifteen and sixteen, then seventeen. Now he was coming in, one final hole, one more par to win it all. The gallery swelled and flowed with his movements, flooding onto the fairway in spite of the efforts of the uniformed guards.

He got the par, a mechanical four.

But there was to be one final incident with dour Ben Hogan. He did not want to affront the British by receiving their most valued trophy in golf without a jacket. So he forced everyone to stand in the rain, cold and shivering, for fifteen minutes while someone went for his coat. Some of the golfers left, and a buzz of indignation rose from the 15,000 massed around the presentation area.

Hogan waited, and when the jacket came, he accepted the trophy from Harry Turcan, the committee chairman at Carnoustie. Ben Hogan had captured the British Open but he had not quite captured the easily-offended British. He was himself—silent and moody—and they wanted him to be chatty and vivacious. He just wasn't that kind of a man. But he did appreciate the gallery and the foreign golfers, and he was heard to murmur "thank you" each time the crowd applauded a good shot.

But Ben Hogan's grand comeback, which had been capped by this tremendous year of 1953, began the day after his accident in 1949. He won the world with his courage and dogged fighting ability, and he inspired admiration for his unflinching, selfless approach to his problems. No one deserved success any more than Ben Hogan, a slight, far-from-powerful golfer who tamed the world's finest with finesse and superb mental application.

The specter of the Hawk marching in solitary dignity down a golf fairway was enough to shake the confidence of other golfers.

"That man," Mangrum has said, "was the only golfer I was truly afraid of," and that sentiment has been echoed by scores of others through the years.

But men who are so tight, so taut, so tense, are often plagued by nerves. Ben could not escape this dread dilemma, and toward the latter part of his career—which, incidentally, has not yet been completed—he admitted a case of "putting nerves" during key moments in pressure tournaments.

In the 1956 U.S. Open in Mamaroneck, New York, Ben needed only two pars on the final pair of holes to tie Cary Middlecoff. But on seventeen he froze on a thirty-incher, suddenly turned, backed off, and waited for a moment. Then he came back and missed it.

"My nerves are shot," he said. "It isn't the legs that go first, it's the nerves."

Another part of the Hogan story that must be told is his personal grief at not being able to win an unprecedented fifth U.S. Open despite several near-misses. He seemed to have it locked up in 1955 at Olympic in San Francisco, when he finished with a 287 only to have a little-known pro named Jack Fleck charge through the final nine to tie him and force a playoff, which Ben lost by three strokes.

On the eighteenth hole of the fourth round, Ben's foot gave way on loose ground and his tee shot hooked into deep, wild rough. When he found the ball, he knew it was trouble come to haunt him again. He took one swing and the ball skidded eighteen inches. Another chop moved it three more feet. He finally reached the fairway on the third try, 100 feet from the green, and was on in five. Then he sank a thirty-foot downhill putt for a six. Fleck was to take a two-putt four on that same hole, good for the tie.

Then came his breakdown in 1956. Again, in 1959, he was in serious contention until he suddenly lost his putting ability and finished five shots behind Billy Casper, the winner.

In 1960 in Denver, he and Arnold Palmer were neck-and-neck until the seventeenth hole of the final day, when a gambling shot missed by six inches, they say, and fell into a water hole. Had the ball hung up on the corner of the green Hogan had aimed for, he could have had his magic fifth.

But the man in the now-famous white cap can be forgiven for this one unfulfilled goal. After all, how many men have won four U.S. Open championships, much less the apparently-unattainable fifth?

The miracle of Ben Hogan's comeback from injury and tragedy can never be diminished, no more than can the unflagging courage he showed during his Hollywood-style battle. The fact that he still plays today (he was an entrant in the $300,000 Dow Jones Open in August of 1970) is a tribute to his talent as well as his charisma. The galleries still follow the Hawk. They love his golf and they love the man.

And no one has ever shown more grit through adversity. When he returned after the accident to play in that Los Angeles Open of 1950, and when he lost out to Snead in the playoff after firing an emotional 280, he won the hearts and the respect of Americans and foreigners alike.

Grantland Rice, the famed sportswriter, in telling of Ben's playoff loss, wrote an immortal line. Speaking of Ben's still-crippled body, his withered legs, and his pain-wracked back, Granny said:

"He lost to Snead because his legs just weren't strong enough to carry his heart."

Ben Hogan did, indeed, have a giant's heart.

CHAPTER FIVE

Arnold Palmer: The Driving Force Behind Golf's Golden Era

CONSIDER, CAREFULLY, THESE NAMES: FRANK STRAFACI, John Veghte, Dick Whiting, Walter Andzel, Frank Stranahan, Don Cherry, Ed Meister, and Bob Sweeny. Put them in a hat and shake well. Ask friends about them. Study them. Find among these amateur golfers of the early and middle 1950's the single overriding denominator they share.

Give up? Well, then, let it be known that these eight men provided victory for Arnold Palmer in the 1954 U.S. Amateur championship played at The Country Club of Detroit in Grosse Point, Michigan. They were his eight victims en route to his first major tournament crown.

The Michigan Eight propelled Arnold Palmer, the Latrobe, Pennsylvania, strongboy, into far more than one amateur championship. They provided the stepping stone from which he went on to build one of golf's all-time fabled careers, and absolutely the most lucrative.

No one then could have ever begun to guess at how far this 25-year-old blond belter would travel. No one would have dared speculate on the impact he was to make on golf in America and over the world. But this was, in truth, Arnie's start—his first major championship—and it was accomplished against a select field of 200 men over six days in August, sixteen golden years ago when another famous golfer, Dwight David Eisenhower, was the President of the United States.

What Arnold Palmer has done for golf and to golf is impossible to judge accurately. But what golf has done for Arnold Palmer is, perhaps, even more difficult to gauge. He made golf a household word and, in return, golf made him a

millionaire several times over. Golf introduced him to celebrities and royalty, presidents and kings, and the beautiful
people of the world. Golf fulfilled dreams no son of a Pennsylvania greenskeeper ever dared dream before. And it made
him the idol of millions.

Arnold Palmer became everyone's Frank Merriwell, and
there had never before been another quite like him. Who is to
say there will ever be another? He took what had been started
by Francis Ouimet, Gene Sarazen, Walter Hagen, Sam Snead,
and Ben Hogan, wrapped it up in golden tinsel, presented it
to the people of the world; and they bought it. He became
Mister Golf.

The spoils of such heroism came fast and furious and are
still flowing. Arnold has made as many millions off the
courses as he earned on them. Arnold Palmer golf equipment
and golf balls, Arnold Palmer putting courses and dry-clean-
ing establishments, have now become familiar and accepted
phenomena throughout the nation. In addition, Arnie has
extensive investments and business dealings in real estate,
securities, and jet airplanes. Finally, he is one of the more
popular celebrities of Madison Avenue, endorsing product
after product to satisfy the hero-worshipping tendencies of
modern America. If the advertised item is good enough for
Arnold Palmer, it is good enough for Everyday Man, and
it doesn't matter if it is a tire, a soft drink, a jacket, or a golf
club. If his name is on it, the product will sell.

But Arnold Palmer could not have accomplished all that is
emblazoned on his record by being simply an accomplished
golfer. Hogan proved that, winning the respect of fans and
golfers but not their adulation. A man must inspire loyalty
and faith, must have that magical quality of charisma. And
Arnold Palmer does have the stuff of which heroes are made.

He is tall and handsome, craggy-faced and broad of shoul-
der, blond and friendly, and muscular enough to attract a
feminine eye. He is far from remote, choosing, rather, to talk

to galleries, to sponsor Arnold Palmer Fan Clubs, to dispense memberships as infantrymen in Arnie's Army, those huge and enthusiastic galleries that dog his steps and intimidate his opponents.

When network television discovered Arnold Palmer, it was a marriage made in heaven, a bond forged of currency and transistor tubes, a union of Madison Avenue with Middle America. His facial expressions during the heat of a tournament range from abysmal depression to unbridled delight. He smokes his cigarette, talks to his fans, and laughs and cheers and hops up and down when a long birdie putt rolls into the cup. He is a joy to televise, they say, because all of America sees something personal in him; the boy next door grown up to be a success . . . the college roommate . . . the forgotten suitor . . . the guy at the next machine on the assembly line.

Yet Arnold Palmer did not spring silver and spoiled from the blueblooded country club set. He is an ordinary man, or was, and he fought his way up—through the days when he worked after school to the times when he drove the tour in a beat-up jalopy, pulling along an ancient trailer for himself and his wife, Winnie, to live in, settling for the $250 prizes for finishing fiftieth until, suddenly, his game was honed and he caught fire, and exploded on the American scene.

And the country was ready for him, for golf had come to occupy a reasonably high place in the realm of sports. But it needed this strong and powerful slugger from the steel mill world of western Pennsylvania to bring it to all the people.

Palmer was golf's first $100,000-plus winner in a single year, and that, like the first four-minute mile, broke the barrier and opened the floodgates for even greater achievements.

The fabulous saga began, professionally, three months after his 1-up victory over Bob Sweeny in the U.S. Amateur Championship of 1954, after he had discussed the idea of playing for money with his dad, Deac Palmer (the greenskeeper and later the pro on the small nine-hole course in Latrobe, about thirty miles from Pittsburgh).

"If I was going to continue playing golf," he recalls, "I thought I might as well do it for a living, too."

And so it was done. Later, when he married Winnie Walzer during the Christmas holidays of 1954, he had been a professional since November 19, the date he signed a contract to endorse a line of items manufactured by a sporting goods company.

"It was rough," he says. "Under PGA rules, I couldn't take any prize money for six months, so I had to scrape. We tried to be available for all the pro-amateur tournaments prior to the big ones, because you could make a couple hundred winning those. Of course, the non-PGA tournaments were very important to us then, too."

But once the six-month probationary period had gone by, things quickly began to fall into place for Arnold Palmer. He won his first tournament—the Canadian Open of 1955—and that year earned $7,958.32 on the tour, enough to rank him thirty-second among leading money-winners and, more important, enough to begin paying the bills and re-paying the loans he and Winnie had made to see them through the early times.

His earnings continued to soar as the tournaments piled up. He won the Insurance City Open and the Eastern Open in 1956 and his earnings mushroomed to $16,144, nineteenth on the list. In 1957 he took the Houston Open, the Rubber City Open, and the San Diego Open and earned $27,802.

Abruptly, his career exploded into nova brilliance the following year. The tournament wins included the Masters, the St. Petersburg Open, and the Pepsi Golf Championship, and he was first on the money list with $42,607. The rest has been all uphill, with one or two minor slumps along the way. Since then, he has added three more Masters victories (1960, 1962, and 1964) and one U.S. Open (1960) that could have been four, since he tied for the lead in 1966 and lost an 18-hole playoff to Billy Casper; tied for the lead in 1962 and lost in a playoff to Jack Nicklaus; and tied in a three-way playoff in 1963 with Jackie Cupit and Julius Boros, the ultimate winner.

Palmer grabbed the British Open in 1961 and 1962, but has never won a PGA championship, a disappointment he is determined to erase before he stops playing on the tour. He was golf's leading money winner four times—1958, 1960, 1962, and 1963. He was voted Pro Player of the Year in 1960 and 1962. He has won the Vardon Trophy four times (1961, 1962, 1964, and 1967), and has been a member of the Ryder Cup team four times (1961, 1963, 1965, and 1967). He was also the team captain in 1963.

It was, perhaps, the Masters victory in 1960 that truly swept Arnold Palmer to the top of the list of the country's golf heroes. His first dramatic charge before a national TV audience was made in that tourney. He was far behind Ken Venturi, both on the scoreboard and on the course, and when Venturi finished with a 283 total he was generally conceded to be the winner. Indeed, he had tried on that traditional green jacket for a fitting, and the TV folks had already begun to brief him on the post-tournament interview procedure.

No one was ready for what Arnie was about to achieve. He approached the seventeenth needing a birdie on the final two holes to gain a tie. No one dared hope for two consecutive birdies on the final two holes of the old Augusta National Course, for they are two of the most difficult finishing holes in the country.

The seventeenth is a 400-yard hole, playing to a par of four. Arnold drove long and right down the middle, then hit an eight-iron to the green, the ball stopping twenty-five feet from the cup. Now the pressure was intense, for the ball should have rolled. Arnie had hit it to roll, but it plopped dead twenty-five feet away. The green was too long, too treacherous, too undulating. Right? Wrong. Not for Arnie, not this day. This day belonged to him.

He lined up the putt, stroked it smartly, and it began its historic roll toward the cup. When it neared the lip, it hesitated for a split second, and Arnie's face muscles knotted into tight bunches as if he were going to push the ball that final inch with his will. Then it fell for a birdie.

Now, of course, a par would gain a tie. It would have been a notable and distinguished achievement. But Arnie was not going to settle for the tie. It is, perhaps, the makeup of the man that dictates boldness when caution is advised, that calls for courage and reckless drive when care is required. No one plays golf exactly the way Arnie Palmer does. That, too, is part of Arnie's mystique.

He stepped up to the tee on the eighteenth and told his caddy about his plans: "No tie. Let's go for the bird."

The eighteenth on the Augusta National Course is a 420-foot par-four devil, seducing the players into a relaxed sensation and then gobbling up iron shots until par is merely hoped for, not expected. But on this day Palmer mastered it with reckless abandon.

He drove into a wind and boomed his shot 260 yards. Approaching the ball, he quickly chose a six-iron and punched a low, fast shot onto the green. It hit, spun, caught, and stopped —five feet from the cup.

Now it was there, the miracle. With millions at home watching in rapt fascination on the TV screens, with Venturi staring morosely at the monitor in the clubhouse, Arnie strode to the ball. He studied it, seemingly at ease, although he later admitted to a writer "it was the most nervous moment in my career." Then, dropping the stub of a cigarette he had been smoking on the green, he hit the ball, and it rolled crisply into the cup. He had won the Masters. He had made a successful charge at a man seemingly home free. It took Arnie over the top.

Afterward, with characteristic irreverence, he set forth his immediate goals. "I want to win a pro's Grand Slam," he stated. "I want to win the Masters, the U.S. Open, the British Open, and the PGA all in a single year. I think that would be a far greater achievement than the Grand Slam scored by Bobby Jones in 1930."

The old guard (and there is a legion of them at Augusta, including Bobby Jones) must have blushed outwardly and grimaced inwardly. But Arnold Palmer spoke with a legion of his own guard behind him. He was secure.

The U.S. Open later that summer provided Arnie's Army with an even greater thrill, from the point of view of the total number of strokes by which he trailed when he began his spirited charge at the leader.

The Open of 1960 was held in June at Cherry Hills Country Club in Denver, Colorado, in the imposing shadow of the snow-capped Rocky Mountains. From the start, Arnie played badly. In addition, he fell victim to some hot shooting by big Mike Souchak. The thin mountain air, likewise, had a bad effect on Palmer, and when he started the first round, his very first shot plunged him into disaster. He was wild at the tee and drove into a ditch. He lifted out, at the cost of a penalty stroke, then hit his third shot short of the green. The fourth shot arched over, and the fifth finally landed near the cup. He holed out for a six, a double bogey.

To his credit, he finished the round with a 72, while Souchak came in with 68, three under par. Mike added a scintillating 67 to his total the next day, and finished the first two rounds with the lowest score ever registered in an Open—135. Palmer? He struggled in with an even-par-71, and was eight strokes off the lead, in fifteenth place. It was an unlikely spot from which to mount a victorious charge.

When Arnie fired a 72 (which included a horrendous double-bogey six on the last hole of the third day) for a 215 total, and Souchak scored a 73 for a 208 aggregate, the situation really looked bleak.

Then on the final day of the tournament Arnie went into

orbit. Five-four-three-two-one . . . ignition. Arnold Palmer took off, and the U.S. Open was his launching pad.

He started the final round with four straight birdies, a string that included a thirty-foot chip shot into the cup on the 410-yard par-four second. He parred the fifth after hitting into the rough, then aroused the crowd by canning his fifth birdie in six holes on the short par-three sixth, snaking a 25-foot putt in from the center of the green—a downhill, curving shot he read perfectly.

On seven he drove the center of the fairway, smacked a wedge shot across a dogleg to within six feet of the cup, and holed out. He was now on a birdie streak of six for the first seven holes, but he went one over par on the eighth by missing a short putt, then took a par on the ninth. Yes, he "took" a par, and he showed displeasure at it.

"I knew," he remarked later, "that I was on my way. After that front nine, I knew I was hitting the ball better than I ever had before."

He had finished the front nine with the incredible score of thirty, the lowest nine-hole score in the history of the U.S. Open, matched only once previously: in 1947, by Jimmy McHale.

Now he turned for home and the electricity crackled all over the course. Fans were running the fairways, cutting across greens, to enlist in Arnie's Army.

Souchak, informed of the dramatic charge, began to crack. He missed an 18-inch putt on the tenth hole and another of a like distance on the eighteenth. He was wilting and Palmer was burning up the course. Mike came in with 75, for a 283, then waited. But there were others who caught fire with Palmer, and the most dramatic finish in Open history up to that time was spilling down the back nine holes.

Jack Fleck took the front nine in 32, but fell back into a tie with Souchak and four others by floating up to bogeys on two of the last three holes. Young Jack Nicklaus had the lead for a brief moment with five under par for the tournament after the 12th, but he took three putts from 10 feet out on the 13th and lost the ball game right there. Bantam Ben Hogan, too, presented a challenge, but on the seventeenth Ben chose to go over a water hazard fronting the green and just missed.

"The shot fell back by inches," said his caddy. "If Mister Ben had made that one, I believe he would have then taken the tournament."

Meanwhile, Arnie kept charging, playing stronger and faster and with mounting confidence as the challengers fell off. He was gaining steam, building up his momentum, and there was no way in the world to cool him off. He scented victory. He knew Souchak's finishing score, and he was confident he could beat that.

On eleven Arnie reached the green of the 563-yard monster in two and required two putts to register another birdie, his seventh of the day. He then put together a string of pars, inflating his score to a back nine of 35 and a torrid 65 for the day. On the final hole he drove off the tee with a one-iron and handled a four-iron like a scalpel, propelling the ball to within 80 feet of the flag. A chip shot grew eyes and came to rest one yard short of the cup, from which point he calmly tapped in the putt for the par and the championship.

He had risen to the challenge of a hopelessly out-of-reach championship, and he had mastered the best in the field. His 280 final total was the best by two strokes, while a young fellow named Jack Nicklaus came in with 282, the lowest score ever registered by an amateur in the tournament. And that includes Bobby Jones.

Thus did the Emperor Arnold begin his reign. He was the undisputed ruler of the world of golf, despite the advance of the young man who would not be denied—Nicklaus. Signing a management contract with a Cleveland lawyer named Mark McCormack, Arnold soon became a millionaire. It did not take long, for the country had fallen under the spell of the Last Minute Hero, and the line of products bearing his name appeared endless. He put his mark on golf shirts, hats, shoes, slacks, jackets, socks, clubs, bags, golf balls and even tees and markers.

He played in lucrative exhibition matches with such men as Gary Player, Jack Nicklaus, Billy Casper, and some of the older, more established players like Sam Snead and Ben Hogan. Soon he was big business, with golf clubs and automobiles and cigarettes and golf carts and a syndicated newspaper instructional clinic to go along with a syndicated newspaper golf column. Palmer was making money so quickly he hired a staff of managers, advisors, and accountants and, perhaps, the business aspect of his life began to press too heavily on his golf game. He went into a slump, but not before playing more topnotch golf.

In 1962 he put on another of his patented charges to tie for the Masters lead after the regulation 72 holes with South African Gary Player. And in the 18-hole playoff the next day, he fell three strokes back after the front nine only to birdie five of the first seven holes coming in and win by three over a suddenly-overcome Player. Overcome? Sure, by the pressure, the strain, and the image of another Palmer charge.

But after that victory, successes in other tournaments became less frequent, and his slump finally evolved into one of pronounced frustration. As with other great golfers who have found tournament victories suddenly elusive, Arnold faulted his putting.

"I haven't putted well since 1960," he moaned during a blow-up in 1963. "I'm fine from tee to green, but I can't put it in the cup any more."

Thus began the undercurrents of whisperings. "He's washed up," they said of the man. "He's making too much money. He doesn't want or care about his golf game any more. He's finished."

But in 1964, Arnold Palmer called a halt to all the wheeling and dealing. He took Winnie and left the tour for a while, and went home to the sprawling ranch house overlooking the course in Latrobe. He began puttering in his shop, tinkering with new club faces, new weight balances, and he practiced. He hit putt after putt after putt. Seldom has a man worked with such determination.

"I heard those rumors, too," he said, "and I did not like them. I wanted to show the people they weren't true."

Later that year he initiated a comeback of sorts, and it began to show. He finished second in six tournaments and third in three, and his earnings, despite the fact that he wasn't winning outright, were just $81 shy of Jack Nicklaus' top figure. Arnold earned $113,203 in 1964, purely from golf purses, and he won the 1964 Masters. His only other tournament victory was the Oklahoma City Open, but he was back, and they all knew it.

And he has stayed back. There have been times when some of the bright promising new players on the tour have upstaged him. He has taken a back seat, on occasion, to people like Nicklaus, Player, Casper, Lee Trevino, Tony Lema, and Frank Beard. But the Master is still Arnold Palmer, as captivating a character as any who ever played this game.

Arnold has registered more individual tournament records than any man, and they have been as diverse and far-ranging as three Texas Opens, three Tournaments of Champions, three Phoenix Opens, and three Los Angeles Opens. He has won the Baton Rouge Open and the Pensacola Open, the Kemper Classic and the Tucson Open, the Insurance City Open, the San Diego Open, and the Thunderbird Open. He has chalked up fifty-four tournament victories since turning pro in 1954, not counting the 1970 season.

He has taken well over $1,000,000 in golf earnings alone, and the fringe income has been many times that but always traces back to the game in its origin. Since 1965 he has not had a year in which he has won less than $100,000 on the tour, capped by an astronomical $184,065 in 1967—which was not enough to top Nicklaus as the leading money winner. Indeed, in point of tournament earnings alone, Nicklaus has won more, and has not been under $100,000 for a single season since 1962.

But much of what the men such as Nicklaus have been able to achieve can be attributed to Palmer. The tournament purses were hiked when Arnie began to work his special magic on nationwide television, so as to insure his presence and the presence, as well, of the all-seeing eye of the on-location camera. If golf can be categorized in its history into three eras, we may point to the impact of Arnold Palmer.

Era One would be the years 1900 through 1925, when the big names were Ouimet, Vardon, Hagen, Ray, and Anderson. There was some money and more prestige, but golf was still a difficult profession for those seeking earnings as well as glory.

Era Two would be from 1925 to the early 1950's, when the big ones were called Hogan, Snead, Sarazen, Armour, Bolt, Harrison, Demaret, and Bobby Jones.

And then there is the Third Era. It starts with Palmer, with his fantastic charges, his impossible finishes, his astronomical earnings. And it takes in all the rest of today's golfers, the top names, the stars, the crowd-magnets. But it starts with Palmer. That is significant. He was the initiating or propelling force of Golf's Golden Era.

What about Arnold Palmer in a more personal, more individual sense? What sort of a man is he? Has he fallen to the temptation of riches and fame? Has he forgotten his beginnings, his friends, his teachers?

Listen to this:

"When things get to be too much, when they get to be tough, I like to pick up and leave the tour for a while. Then we go home to Latrobe and I fool around with the caddies, and I knock around some clubs in the shop and I play a little golf with the local guys. It relaxes me.

"I don't much like the daily pressures of tournament golf, and I'm not crazy about dressing up all the time for parties and personal appearances. I am pleased to death that I am such a very special favorite with the people of this country, but I'm sure they understand that you can't sign autographs and make television shows all the time.

"After a while, I just have to get away, to walk around in old shoes and wrinkled slacks and a sweater and stay at home and relax. I think all this success came so fast for me that I never learned how to feel comfortable with it. I'm still a plain country guy, and I like the plain things.

"Dinner alone with Winnie, playing friendly golf, working in the pro shop, tinkering with clubs . . . that's where it's all at for me. I hope I never lose my taste for that, because that is the real life, those are the things that are important. The rest is great, but golf gave it to me, and I still like to think I'm a regular guy who just happened to play a couple of good rounds of golf."

So speaks Arnold Palmer, the King of Golf.

He is far from an ordinary man, and this might be realized with a touch of sadness on his part. He still feels he is just another guy who started to play golf. The modesty is another characteristic of the man. It is, perhaps, the one reason why he has remained human and friendly and affable throughout his incredible career.

He has had his ups and downs, but there have been more of the ups. For this he is grateful. And so is golf.

CHAPTER SIX

Jack Nicklaus: The Golden Bear

WHEN HE FIRST BEGAN TO TEAR UP THE COUNTRY'S MOST ruthless courses, they called him The Bear. Then, when he not only won their biggest tournaments but began making money with the same speed as his titanic swing of a driver, they changed that. They called him The Golden Bear.

Meet Jack Nicklaus.

No one hits the ball further off the tee, or higher and straighter, with more consistency. No one has his game so finely tuned to the power lurking in his massive arms and shoulders. No one has been able to master courses as he has with his sheer strength. No one, perhaps not even Arnold Palmer, will make as much money from tournament purses.

And very few of the world's all-time best golfers were as ready to play championship golf at such an early age as Jack Nicklaus, the Golden Bear from Columbus, Ohio.

Nicklaus turned pro in 1962, having established himself as National Amateur king twice in three years. The first major tournament he entered as a pro was the U.S. Open. He won it. Within two short years, he had taken the nation's top three championships—the Open, the Masters, and the PGA. He has won many tournaments, but not as many as Palmer. Yet he has been a professional seven fewer years.

But his money winnings have even now reached an astronomical level—higher than Palmer's. He has been either first or second in the annual money sweepstakes all but two of the years he has been a pro. Once, in his first year, he was third; in 1969, he was sixth. In 1964 and 1965, he was the back-to-back money leader, taking away sums of $113,284 and $140,752 from the courses. In 1967, when he again was the top money winner, his earnings reached a lofty $188,998.

Perhaps his most consistent attribute, however, is the fact that he has won more than $100,000 for seven consecutive years.

Nicklaus has accomplished what Palmer has thus far failed to do—win a PGA title. He has three Masters victories to his credit (in 1963, 1965, and 1966) and two U.S. Opens (1962 and 1967). He teamed with Palmer to win the 1966 PGA team championships, and it was undoubtedly the most awesome, booming duo to ever attack an underdog golf course.

In 1967, when Nicklaus won his second U.S. Open at the Baltusrol Golf Club in Springfield, New Jersey, he did so with a tournament record score of 275. In 1965, when he won his second Masters, he did so with a "miracle" score of 271, a full 17 strokes under par. That four-round set prompted Bobby Jones to call the tournament "the greatest performance in the history of golf tournaments."

There is nothing that Nicklaus has not won. No major tournament has eluded the grasp of his pudgy fingers. No praise has been denied him. His golf game, perhaps not as stylish as that of Snead, Hogan, Hagen, or Sarazen, has been lauded as "the most powerful in the world." Nicklaus does not bother to consider the fine points of a course.

"I do not commit a course to memory," he said. "I do not memorize the traps and the distances and the little secrets golfers think they find. I write down those things. Then I go out and just hit 'em."

If Jack Nicklaus was young as a champion (he is only 30 today), then he was young merely in years. In experience, he was a seasoned veteran. He had played golf—sub-par, professional-type golf—since his early teens. It was the game he chose, by himself, and it was the game he decided he could master.

It all began for Nicklaus in 1959, when, as a brash nineteen-year-old, the blond, round-cheeked, apple dumpling from Ohio won the National Amateur with a 1-up victory over Charlie Coe. He was prevented from defending his championship the following year, when Charles Lewis beat him in the fifth round at the St. Louis Country Club. But in 1961, as a "grown man" of 21, he absolutely devastated Dudley Wysong, 8 and 6, to regain the title.

Then he decided to turn pro, disappointing those who had already begun to think of him as the top amateur, those who had publicly stated that this husky boy was capable of achieving even more as an amateur than the immortal Bobby Jones. It is true that, in 1960, he finished second to Palmer in the U.S. Open at the Cherry Hills Country Club in Denver by two strokes, with a 282 total that was a tournament record for an amateur. And it is further true that the following year, at the Oakland Hills Country Club in Birmingham, Michigan, he shot a 284 to finish in a tie for third with Mike Souchak, three strokes behind Gene Littler, the winner.

But the lure of the folding green had become paramount in Nicklaus' mind.

"If I was playing that well, I thought I might as well get paid for it," he said. "I wasn't born a rich kid. Money like they were offering on the tour seemed like all the money in the world."

So the son of the Columbus druggist left the world of the amateur and leaped feet-first into the jungle of the play-for-pay stylists.

They never had a chance.

The 1962 U.S. Open was held at the Oakmont Country Club in Oakmont, Pennsylvania, from June 14 through 17. It was Arnold Palmer's home course, and never was Arnie's Army more exuberant. Nicklaus was young and relatively obscure to most golf fans, and, of course, totally unknown to members of Arnie's Army.

But Jack Nicklaus, who had said quite bluntly "I want to

be the best golfer this world has ever seen," was ready for the test. He did not even consider the odds against him, the odds that would have called his chances impossible. He was a boy in his first big tournament, up against the country's top golfers in what many feel is the most important and meaningful tournament in the nation.

"I could win it," Nicklaus had said, and people would have laughed had they heard him. But Jack Nicklaus did not attract much attention then. He had to prove himself first.

Jack drew Palmer as his playing partner for the first two rounds, and to be forced to go around with that pack of fans baying at their heels has broken the game of many older and more experienced players. But Nicklaus, who has the happy facility of being able to retreat within himself in pressure moments, acted as though there was no noise, no boisterous yells, no rude and intentional sudden sounds when he got ready to putt. He just played the course.

"I had been at Oakmont since that Monday," he says, "and I had played some practice rounds. It's a big sucker of a course, but I decided I could control it. I decided to hit everything just as hard as I could, because it was easier for me to go over the trouble spots than to go around them."

His first round was a 72. Palmer came in with 71, and the early leader became Gene Littler, with a 69.

Nicklaus' second round was good for a 70. But Arnie toured in a scintillating 68. The 139 tied Arnie at the halfway point with Bob Rosburg, while Nicklaus was at 142, three away.

Then they played the third round, and Arnie registered a scrambling 73. Nicklaus shaved a stroke off his lead by firing a 72, while Rosburg made a rapid exit as a serious contender. Later that day (for they still played the final 36 holes on the final day, a Saturday) Nicklaus and Palmer, who had changed partners, nevertheless neared the confrontation with each other. Arnie held a two-stroke advantage over the burly Bear, but Jack was advancing in his slow, methodical manner, and it was imperative that Arnie stay clear of trouble. He did not.

Instead, needing a par-five on the ninth hole in the final round, he drove into the rough and had to pitch back to the fairway. But he misread the height of the grass, flubbed the shot and the ball inched forward perhaps ten to twelve feet.

He had to take a six, while Nicklaus played the same ninth hole in par. Then, on eleven, Jack holed out from fourteen feet for a birdie, thus moving within one stroke of his rival. He evened matters on thirteen when Palmer bogeyed. Jack was still imperturbable, shooting par after par, with an occasional birdie when he felt the distance was right for a boomer.

Now it was even and both men played par the rest of the way home. Jack had two-putted on eighteen, giving Palmer one final shot at the championship outright. Arnie had a twelve-foot putt for a birdie, and it would have won the tournament. But he did not get it, the ball barely eluding the outstretched lip of the cup (it was, after all, Arnie's home course) and they were tied.

An eighteen-hole playoff was necessary, to be held the following day, Sunday. Jack had played the final 18 in 69; Palmer in 71. The men who work for the TV networks were beside themselves with glee. Palmer, the hero to millions, matched against the chunky giant-killer of a boy for the U.S. Open championship.

A gigantic crowd appeared for the playoff. It was a deliriously pro-Arnie crowd. But Nicklaus was unmoved.

"Nobody figured me to win anyway," he later said, "so I figured I had no reason to play scared or cautious. They all thought Palmer would win it. I had nothing to lose."

Nothing, that is, except the U.S. Open crown. But Jack knew what he could do. He was his own man.

Palmer took a bogey-five on the first hole. Jack parred it. They stayed that way until the fourth, a par-five, 544-yard mankiller. Jack was out-driven (for the first time) off the tee, and then he hit into the rough. A three-iron brought him safely onto the fairway but in an extremely difficult position in relation to the green, which was one hundred yards away and protected by a gaping, yawning trap.

Jack called on his power, on his range with irons, and he exploded a wedge shot that cleared the sand, sped true for the pin, and stopped six feet away. The birdie putt was child's play for him.

Arnie parred the hole, and he was down by two.

Four more holes were played, and Jack picked up two more strokes; after eight, with ten to play, the boy was leading Arnold Palmer by four strokes. He was putting superbly, and his drives were traveling farther and higher than fans in those parts could recall. He was also a silent rock of strength, apparently immune to the unfair pressure applied by the vocal chords of Arnie's Army.

Then Palmer, who seemed hopelessly out of it, suddenly made his charge. The electricity caught the crowd, which had been hoping for such magic, and ignited the course in a flash fire of optimism.

"Arnie's doing it, he's charging," they cried, and the jostling for position became even wilder.

Arnie birdied the ninth, the eleventh, and the twelfth. He picked up a stroke on each hole, since Nicklaus could not escape the par rut, and now he trailed by one.

Then, on thirteen, Arnie fell short on his iron tee shot, and since the green was barely 161 yards away, the pin was set well back on the green. Palmer's shot barely hung to the corner of the green, and he found three putts were necessary to hole out. He had bogeyed, while Jack parred and went ahead by two. The charge was nipped, strangled. They played par until eighteen, where Palmer, gambling on big shots, bogeyed for a final round total of 74.

Jack? He was still poker-faced, still calm and cool, still shooting par golf. He came in with a 71 and had become the

Open champ, the youngest to hold that distinction since
Bobby Jones in 1923.

He had beaten the best in a select field and even that had
not given him the championship outright. Then he had to take
the measure of Mister Golf, Arnold Palmer, in a pressure-
packed 18-hole playoff, where the intensity of the competition reaches crucible heat, where the tension hangs in the air,
where six-foot putts seem six miles long, where you can hear
the whole world breathing in your ear.

"It was kind of satisfying," young Jack Nicklaus said, later.

Although he was not to win another Open until five years
later—the record 275 at Baltusrol—Nicklaus had established a
firm niche for himself among the leaders of the new gener-
ation of golf stars. His power was impossible for the old-
timers to match. When good drives were once 200 to 225
yards, Nicklaus was able to do that with irons. He drove
consistently in the 275-to-285-yard class, and more than a few
times reached 300 yards, making all courses easy to tame. Going over trouble on the fly is ideal, but very few were capable of it.

In the years after that marvelous Open victory of 1962,
Nicklaus became golf's new hero. His winnings—$61,868 for
his first year, 1962—were enough to rank him third among
all the pros. He reached the $100,000 level in 1963, with such
victories as the Masters and the PGA, the Palm Springs Classic, the Tournament of Champions, and the Sahara Invitational—five major tournament laurels to pile up in his rec
room.

He won only four tournaments in 1964, but finished near
the top in so many others that his earnings ($113,284) led the
nation's pros. He took the Tournament of Champions for a
second straight year, along with the Phoenix and Portland
Opens and the Whitemarsh Classic in Philadelphia. And how
did the Golden Bear fare in 1965? Very well, thanks. He
again led the country's golfers in the money sweepstakes,

taking down prizes worth $140,752, and winning such events as the Masters, the Portland Open, the Memphis Open, the T-Bird Classic, and the Philadelphia Classic.

Continuing to build his fortune, and establishing his off-the-course income with endorsements and business ventures, Nicklaus sped through 1966 as the scourge of the courses. He "slumped" in money won from purses, down to $111,419, which was good enough only for second place, but the tournaments he won included the Masters (for a second year in a row), the Sahara Invitational, and the PGA team championship, with Palmer.

Then came 1967 and the U.S. Open record and what he has often called "my best tournament, considering everything." It was as if he hit each and every shot the way the course designer had intended. The drives were, it seemed, longer and higher than ever before. His iron shots were perfect, bold and straight and close to the pin. His putting was nerveless. He never seemed to waver, never hesitated. He took his time—indeed, Nicklaus has become known as one of the slowest, most maddening putters on the tour—but he hit each ball with the precise strength necessary. He read each green as though he had planted the grass himself.

There is more to the Jack Nicklaus story, but it has yet to unfold. The Golden Bear has won every major tournament within the scope of professional golf, but there is a good deal more in store. How many times will he be able to repeat in his tour victories? How much money will he be able to wring from the tournament purses? Will he break all the old barriers? Will he, for instance, win five Opens? Five PGA's? Five Masters? Will he eventually earn more than $2,000,000 from tour prizes? It did not seem possible before he started playing; now it seems almost inevitable.

Nicklaus has become equally famous for his stature as an international golfer. In 1963, playing as a twenty-three-year-old in the British Open at St. Anne's-on-the-Sea in England, he needed only to play par over the final two holes to win, but he missed out by one stroke when he bogeyed each of the finishers. So in 1966 he went back and won it. He has also garnered the Canada Cup International Trophy, in Paris in 1963.

Some treatment of Nicklaus's character is needed here, for those who have seen fit to demean his attitude on the course and off it.

"He won too much too soon," the detractors chirp, "and he just does not care any longer about his golf. He takes his time and he is without emotion. It looks as though he lacks concentration and determination."

It is, of course, an unfair and inaccurate charge. But it does stem from some puzzling behavior which must be explained. On the course, no matter what the tournament, no matter how intense the pressure, Jack Nicklaus smiles and grins and seems without care. It is his makeup. He does not attempt to hide it, but he becomes annoyed when his outward appearance is used to detract from his character.

"Competitive spirit is something inside a man," he says. "People are different and their makeups are different, and this is mine. I don't think I could change it if I tried, and I don't think I would care to try. It has worked for me. Sure, I get as nervous before and during a major tournament as anyone. But, I guess, it just doesn't show on me. That does not mean I'm loafing or lackadaisical. It's just the way I am. I think I want to win tournaments—the big ones and the rest, too—as much as the next guy.

"I just can't help it if I don't show my feelings on the outside. If I don't set my jaw and jangle my change and tug at my hat, it doesn't mean I don't care. It doesn't mean I don't have the desire. It's just my way. Golf is my life, and I am not going to have anybody tell me how to run it or how to behave. There is no proper way. I just do it my way."

Many golfers have become known for their behavior on

the course during a tournament. Hogan was the solitary man, needing and heeding no one. Palmer is outgoing and friendly, chatting with the gallery, with his caddy—until it becomes tough. Then he does set his jaw, and he tugs at his trousers, and becomes silent.

Lee Trevino has become known for his excitement, which he seems to bring to each major event. He is brash and cocky and fun-loving, and he inspires the same sort of hero-worship, albeit not as extensive, as Palmer. "Lee's Fleas" have become the answer to Arnie's Army, but Trevino has his more serious moments, especially during the final round of a tournament in which he is in serious contention.

Doug Sanders, with his famous flamboyant manner of dressing, is another extrovert who can suddenly clam up when the going gets tough. Gary Player is known for his all-black clothing on the course, for his polite but firm avoidance of many of the pre- and post-tournament social events. Billy Casper won the following of many Americans who sympathized with his overweight problem and who were intrigued by the exotic qualities of his "doctor imposed" diets. Bear steak, indeed.

Perhaps Nicklaus' point is that it is an emotional chore to turn on the charm while playing, and then just as suddenly to shut it off when the tension rises. Perhaps, in his placid, never-hear-a-thing fashion, he is more relaxed than those players who must be constantly changing their moods as the tempo of the tournament changes.

When the PGA put its anti-slowdown rulings into effect, Nicklaus was one of the most vehemently opposed to the regulations. His game is one of patience and certainty. He has made a habit of "charting" a course during the practice rounds which he feels are an absolute necessity prior to the start of a tournament. But, unlike Hogan and Snead, he does not commit vital statistics to memory. He writes all vital statistics on slips of paper: the distance from a trap to the green, the various yard measurements he feels are necessary to play the course properly, the distinguishing characteristics of a green, a hazard, or a patch of rough. And he keeps the slips of paper tucked away in a back pocket for reference during the tournament rounds.

Such a practice, understandably, can irritate those he is playing with and those immediately behind him, as well as the often-stuffy PGA officials who patrol the courses and constantly check on the contestants. Jack has been known to walk off half the distance of a fairway, to check on a measurement, before striding back and hitting the ball. But the annoyance and the exasperation of his opponents has unflaggingly failed to change his approach or hurry his play.

"It is my way," he repeats, "and I do not intend to be told how to play my kind of golf."

Jack is also a sensitive man, though not as much now as he was when he first exploded on the pro tour. His weight has been a source of embarrassment to him. While at Ohio State, the 220-pounder was called a variety of none-too-genteel names by classmates—names such as "Whaleman," "Blobbo," and "Jelly." When he first began playing with the men, he was quickly christened "Ohio Fats." He never protested, but he has admitted to friends that it does bother him.

However, he insists he feels "stronger" at his current weight, which can fluctuate from 205 to 220 pounds. And when Jack is strong, the drives soar far and true and that, really, is what Nicklaus's game is all about.

Young Jack Nicklaus came from a sports-minded family and began to play golf while he was still in his early teens. His father, L. Charles Nicklaus, was a three-sports (football, baseball, basketball) standout at Ohio State. He played professional football with the Portsmouth Spartans, and he had established scoring records on the municipal golf course in Columbus, Ohio—where he played only on weekends.

Jack, too, became a sports fan early, and participated in all of the games played in the parks and playgrounds.

But golf soon became his favorite, and he began swinging clubs with his awesome power on the Scioto Club course, famed for hosting several major tournaments including many U.S. Open championships.

As a lad of ten, Jack shot a nine-hole round of 51, and was regularly beating the local duffers by the time he was in his early teens. The pro at Scioto at the time was Jack Grout, who enrolled Jack in several classes because he saw some of the potential in the swing and putting ability of this young giant. It was Grout who instructed Nicklaus to hit with power every time, on every shot.

"Just hit it out of trouble and don't worry about how you look," he suggested, somewhat unorthodox in his advice but totally practical when aimed at such a find.

Jack was a quick and apt pupil, learning as fast as Grout could instruct, taking it all in because of his fascination with the game.

"Even then," Grout recalls, "you could see that he had a chance to be special. I never saw a kid hit a ball that far and that hard."

Nicklaus soon became too much for Grout to contend with, for he was breaking 80 by the time he was thirteen and, at sixteen, won the Ohio Open, finishing ahead of several notable pros in the process. He was on his way.

During the amateur portion of his career, he qualified for the U.S. Amateur championship seven times and, of course, won the tournament twice, in 1959 and 1961. His first appearance was in 1955, at the tender age of fifteen, and it was then that he first met Bobby Jones, a man with whom he was soon to be favorably compared as both a champion and a child star.

The Amateur tourney of that year was held at the Country Club of Virginia in Richmond, and Bobby Jones made the trip for the primary reason of watching this prodigy in action. He joined the gallery which had begun to follow this incredibly long-hitting man-child.

"On the eleventh tee, I saw him in the crowd," Jack recalls, "and I started getting all shaky. I was so excited I hooked my drive into the woods. Then I overpowered a chip shot and drove over the green on the thirteenth. I was so nervous I don't remember if I even held the clubs properly. Then I saw him head back to the clubhouse, and I felt terrible."

But Jones had seen enough. He said that, while he saw some bad shots, he was impressed with the youngster's power and swing, and soon became one of his most ardent supporters. Indeed, Jones has admitted—and Jack has corroborated—that he wrote a letter to Nicklaus some years later, strongly urging him against turning professional.

At the age of 19 Nicklaus was elected to the U.S. Walker Cup, and he ignited a 9-3 victory over the British at Muirfield, Scotland. He won both his matches, against older and far more seasoned performers. His fame as an amateur grew with each victory, and during the year of 1959 he lost only one of thirty matches played.

Then, two years later, he won the Amateur again and shortly thereafter decided to play professionally.

"I know I disappointed a lot of people," he later admitted, "but I didn't know what to do. Everything had happened so fast I was confused. I was still trying to earn my degree from Ohio State. I had an insurance business I was trying to get off the ground. And I was playing golf all the time. Finally, I decided I had to choose, and I chose to devote all my time to the golf."

It was a move that Jones, especially, greeted with sadness. But this was a different era, an era in which the riches of the tour were far greater than in the days of the 1920's and 1930's, when Jones was famed as an amateur who could play better than any of the existing pros. It was a choice made with his family in mind, a choice based on practicality. He has never had reason to regret it—and neither has the world of golf. Perhaps only the other pros, who also must earn a living, have felt twinges of regret that Jack Nicklaus failed to remain an amateur.

"I just hate to play that big, happy kid," Arnold Palmer has often said, in a voice that blends envy with good humor.

CHAPTER SEVEN

Ken Venturi and the 1964 U.S. Open

KEN VENTURI HAS BEEN HARDENED BY TRAGEDY, HIS SPIRIT steeled by the weight of misfortune.

From the height of a brilliant early career he was carried down by adversity, almost eliminated from golf. He had to beg for invitations to tournaments where the directors once beseeched him to enter. He suffered through a long and seemingly never-ending drought, when he won virtually nothing and inherited the legacy of failure each time he tried to change his luck.

Ken Venturi has been plagued by personal tragedy, both to himself and his family. He has undergone several episodes of major surgery in an attempt to correct and relieve nerve pressure that caused a circulatory ailment in his hands, a numbness in his wrists, a near-paralysis of his right side. He lingered through the long and terrible hours of a post-accident operation on his son, Timmy, then seven, in 1966. Timmy had been riding his bicycle when the gate hook of a passing truck caught him in the mouth and ripped out half his face.

Through plastic surgery and modern medicine, the boy escaped permanent injury or disfigurement, but for Venturi, the accident and its worrisome aftermath were nerve-shaking experiences to further try his soul.

Ken Venturi's career began with incandescent brilliance when as a young and brash golfer, he challenged, and often defeated, the best of the pros. Then his luck turned and, for a while, he seemed destined to finish in the grayness of a forgotten man. In 1963, for example, he started in twenty-seven tournaments and finished no higher than 18th in any of them. He collected prize money in only eight, and his winnings for the year amounted to a paltry $3,848. Two years before he had won $25,572. In 1958, his second year on the tour, he had won $36,267. Indeed, he had taken home $18,761 in his first professional season.

Then, miraculously, 1964 arrived for Ken Venturi.

"If I ever needed a break," Venturi remembers, "it was then. That year I was at my lowest point. I had to get some encouragement, somewhere, from someone, or I would have dropped from golf. I was depressed and my physical problems began to become mental ones. I was scared to play golf for fear I'd blow up again, and when I played scared, I blew up."

In January, 1964, seeking a new start and finally cured of his pinched nerve ailment, Ken Venturi set out to recapture the old magic. His game was sound and he was hitting straight again, but he missed the cut in the Los Angeles Open and in the Bing Crosby Open, and went home to San Francisco to practice and to think. Mostly to think.

"My confidence was shot," he admitted. "I didn't know if I could play golf any more. I had to try it by myself before I would go back out there." Out there meant the tour. A tour he had once come close to dominating.

Ken Venturi, born on May 15, 1931, in San Francisco, had turned to the professional life in 1956, and in his first two years he won six major tournaments. In the first four years he won ten. Among the more renowned and lucrative were the St. Paul Open of 1957, the T-Bird Invitational and the Phoenix Open of 1958, the Los Angeles Open and his second consecutive Gleneagles-Chicago Open of 1959, the Bing Crosby National Invitational, and the Milwaukee Open of 1960.

He was runner-up to Arnold Palmer in the 1960 Masters. He was young and bright and promising, and the golf community parted when he arrived, making a path for this talented newcomer.

The problems began in 1962, early in the year, while he was playing in the Palm Springs Classic. He suffered a pinched nerve in his side, a painful and long-lasting condition that nearly paralyzed his right side, made it practically impossible for him to lift his right arm, and sent shooting pains down his back, his legs, and into his chest.

He sought medical help, but cortisone shots, pain-killers, whirlpool baths, and heat treatments only dispelled the pain slowly. He spent two solid years, 1962 and 1963, vainly searching for a tournament victory, while his earnings for those years dropped drastically. In 1962 he earned $6,951. In 1963, as previously mentioned, the total was $3,848. He had, for all intents and purposes, disappeared as a factor of any kind on the tour.

After returning from his traumatic two-tournament tour in early 1964, he went to an old friend and confidante, Byron Nelson. The one-time magician of the courses had remodeled Venturi's game twice before, back in 1952 and 1955. On the first occasion, Nelson had asked Ken to play a round with him, and Venturi toured the 18 holes in a scintillating 66.

"Meet me here tomorrow morning," Nelson said brusquely. "There are half a dozen things you are doing wrong. I'll fix them for you."

Venturi did not know it, of course, but the old pro bothered to coach only those he felt could become outstanding golfers. Venturi was one of those.

Nelson went to work on Ken's unorthodox grip, in which he allowed too much play with the handles of the clubs. He straightened out his swing and he repositioned Venturi's feet on iron shots. Ken proved a quick learner, and soon was Nelson's pride and joy.

When Venturi entered the Army, in 1953, he stopped playing competitive golf. Two years later, after his discharge, Nelson worked with him again. Then early in 1956, Ken became one of 42 amateurs invited to play in the venerable Masters tournament, a competition no amateur had ever won before.

Ken Venturi made the course seem simple. He started with a first round 66 and held that lead through three rounds. He was the leader with half a dozen holes left to play on the final day. And then he blew; he exploded his game all over the course and when they picked up the pieces he had shot an 80 and lost the tournament by one stroke to Jack Burke.

It was Venturi's bitter contention afterward that he had been jobbed. He had been set to play with his old coach, Nelson, on the final day of the tournament. But Bobby Jones and Cliff Roberts, the two men who rule the Masters, decided this student-teacher relationship might be construed as a conflict of interests. Instead, Venturi was paired off with Sam Snead, who was in the running and who, of course, offered nothing but silence to this young phenom.

Venturi's reaction was not taken easily by the rest of the pros on the tour. Ken quickly became controversial, and found it difficult to get along with the other stars. But that was Venturi. He spoke his mind and he did not stop to consider any possible repercussions. Right or wrong, he was his own master.

"If I said it, I must have meant it," he said later. "Otherwise, I wouldn't have said it. I stated then that I thought I was treated unfairly in that tournament and I would say it again today if I had to. I believed it."

After practicing and thinking during the spring of 1964, Ken decided to take one more crack at the pro tour. He received the last invitation to the $100,000 Thunderbird Open because he called and requested it. Then he finished in a tie for fifth, with winnings of $6,250—more than he had won during all of the preceding year. Then he qualified for the Open by shooting 147 in a sectional tournament—a 70 in the second round to pull him past 45 others.

He was ready for history's touch.

The 1964 U.S. Open was played at the Congressional Country Club just outside Washington, D.C. The course (7,053 yards) was the longest in the history of the tournament that was inaugurated in 1895. That, however, was far from the only problem Congressional and its environs presented.

The traps were treacherous and the greens undulated to the tune of a siren's song. But perhaps the worst problem of all was the heat. A murderous heat wave had blanketed the entire area with thick layers of humid, blazing-hot air. The humidity sapped strength and concentration, tugged at the fatigue strings of men, and affected scores of otherwise reliable shotmakers.

Venturi fired a 72 for the first round, which was played in a muggy furnace of 90 degrees. Palmer had a 68, and Nicklaus, with Arnie the other co-favorite, tied Venturi. The scores of the rest of the contestants had been inflated by the difficult conditions and Nicklaus, for example, was to go through one of those infrequent tournaments in which he was literally no factor.

The second day dawned as hot and as muggy as the first, and Venturi added a 70 while Palmer backed his 68 with an equally stellar 69. But a twenty-nine-year-old pro named Tommy Jacobs, who teed off early in the morning and was in by noon, soared into contention with a 64. The score, which included six birdies and a dozen pars, was a tournament round record shared by Lee Mackey, Jr., who had done it fourteen years earlier at the Merion Cricket Club.

As they prepared for the final, brutal day of 36 holes, Jacobs held the lead with 136, a single stroke ahead of Palmer, and a full six strokes in front of Venturi. It seemed hopeless, impossible to catch the leaders, particularly when Saturday arrived with all the friendliness of a thermometer gone berserk. Slowly the mercury crept upward until it touched the 100-degree mark. Fans in the galleries were treated for heat exhaustion. Perspiration turned clothing into sodden lumps of fabric.

Palmer was in trouble from the start, scrambling and scratching on each hole. He settled for a morning round of 75, while Jacobs turned in a 70. And when they broke for lunch, they discovered that Ken Venturi had shot a near-impossible 66. He was suddenly up there, two strokes behind Jacobs, four ahead of Palmer, with eighteen left to play. But it was a cruel and vicious day, and the morning eighteen had already taken its toll of the golfers.

Palmer returned to the clubhouse pale and drawn; Jacobs had a harried, exhausted appearance; and Venturi, who had neglected to eat breakfast or to take the precious, badly-needed salt tablets, was nearly unconscious.

But his round that morning belied his fatigue. He rolled in one birdie putt after another, sinking his longest on the eighth hole—from 25 feet away.

"I was shaking so badly," Venturi recalled, "that I could barely hold my putter. But I knew it wasn't nerves or my old problem, because I was shaking all over."

And then Joe Dey, the executive director of the USGA, needing only a cursory glance to see the seriousness of Venturi's condition, called for Dr. John Everett, a club member. He asked Dr. Everett to follow Venturi around for the final eighteen holes; he went along to condone, unofficially, the slow pace at which Venturi had to play, adding yet further drama to the courageous performance this man, who had been down and out, was putting on.

During lunch, Dr. Everett ordered Venturi to bed. He fed him tea and salt tablets, nothing more. And when they went back out into the blast furnace, Dr. Everett maintained a con-

stant vigil over his patient, a man, who, by all rights, should
have been in a hospital but instead was playing eighteen more
murderous holes in search of the U.S. Open championship.
Venturi was close to fainting when he started to play. At
times he stopped dead still on the course, as if trying to mar-
shal the strength to go on. Several times Dr. Everett handed
him a plastic bag of ice to hold against his forehead.

"If he was a fighter," the doctor said, "I would have
stopped the fight. He was in no condition to walk, let alone
play golf."

But play golf he did, and somehow Venturi's game was not
affected by his tenuous physical condition. Time after time
he began weaving, as if preparing to faint, and each time he
righted himself. He parred the first five holes, three-putted
the sixth for a bogey, but birdied the seventh to get back to
par for the round. Jacobs, meanwhile, was experiencing trouble and was three over par after the first two holes. Venturi
had it, and when Jacobs rang up bogeys again on the ninth
and tenth, all Ken had to do was play par golf.

But, in truth, all he had to do was find the inner fortitude
to finish. It boiled down to that. If he could finish, the Open
was his. But there was a real and serious doubt that he could
finish.

On the thirteenth hole Venturi somehow tapped in a putt
from eighteen feet away, and he now led by four strokes,
a margin he was to maintain to the breath-taking, nerve-
wracking finish.

As he approached the eighteenth green, hiking over a steep
hill on which he twice stumbled and nearly fell, Dey said to
him: "Hold your head up, Ken. You're the champion now."

As if overhearing his words, the crowd that lined both
sides of the fairway began to applaud, hesitantly at first, then
building to a tumultuous crescendo. Venturi doffed his cap
and waved it to the crowd. Then he putted out from ten feet
away for a par-four and the championship. It was a round of

70 and it built his winning score to 278, second only to the 276 shot by Ben Hogan sixteen years earlier at the Riviera Country Club in Los Angeles.

Then Ken Venturi went back to the cooler confines of the clubhouse and collapsed.

"When I won the Open," Venturi said later, "I found that my entire outlook on golf was changed. I wasn't afraid of the big tournaments any longer. I actually looked forward to them. My attitude changed, too.

"I stopped thinking about the traps and the bunkers," Ken added, as if glorying in his new-found confidence. "I started to think only about where the pins were. I was shooting for the pins, not worrying about what lay between the tee and the green. It was as if I had lifted a curtain from in front of my eyes. I began to enjoy golf again, and I feel you must enjoy anything in order to do it well."

Ken Venturi suffered a relapse of his circulatory trouble, and soon he slumped again—this time, very badly. His earnings for 1964, the Year of the Open, had soared to $62,465. But suddenly, almost without warning, he fell from sight. He earned the grand total of $295 the next year, managed a small recovery in 1966 when he won the Lucky International (for him, a most fittingly named tournament) and earned a gross of $21,226. But then he dropped from the tour for all of 1967 and 1968, a troubled man, a man with problems that were physical in origin but began to sap his confidence once more. He was plagued by doubt—doubt about his hands, the deeper nature of his illness, and his ability to play golf again.

He played in 1969, but did not fare well at all. In the list of the world's money winners, the name Ken Venturi, to one scanning the roster, does not appear until the 179th spot. It shows him having earned $7,628, just ahead of a Japanese professional named Takashi Murakami, who managed to collect $7,561.

And now the future holds nothing but clouds for Ken

Venturi. He does not know if he can ever regain the magic of the irons and the accuracy of his putting. At age 39, this could well be his final chance to mount yet another comeback. This could be it for Ken Venturi.

But should that unfortunate possibility bear fruit, should this man who was once considered to be the brightest of new stars never again play on the tour, what he accomplished in 1964 will stand always as his finest moment.

Ken Venturi was, in every sense of the word, an ingenue. The emotionalism of his victory in the 1964 Open was, in part, the story of his spotty career. He had caught the eye of a San Francisco auto dealer named Eddie Lowery, the very same Lowery who, years before, had played hooky from school to caddy for a 20-year-old former caddy named Francis Ouimet in the 1913 U.S. Open. Lowery, who was eventually to sponsor Venturi, thought he had found a new champion.

"He was shooting very well, breaking into the 70's," Lowery recalls, "without knowing exactly what he was doing. I was never a very good golfer myself, but I knew what good golfers—no, great golfers—were supposed to look like. And Venturi had that look."

National junior championships were in store for the young Venturi when he was seventeen, and then, at eighteen, he won the San Francisco City Open, the youngest player to ever do so. Lowery decided he had better seek more professional guidance for the budding star, and he arranged that momentous meeting with Byron Nelson.

The two became fast friends, Nelson teaching, Venturi following each instruction to the letter. By the time Byron felt he had taught his pupil all he could, he was envious of the way Venturi played his irons, for example.

"He hit them better and with more distance and accuracy than I ever did," Nelson said, and coming from one of the all-time greats that was no small compliment.

Then came his two-year service in the Army, with Nelson waiting to polish up the boy's game upon his discharge.

"He didn't really lose anything," Nelson remembered. "He just had been away from the game for so long that he needed to re-learn some of the things a man doesn't lose if he plays competitively. It was a refresher course, I suppose, and it all came back to him very quickly."

Then Venturi entered the 1956 Masters and lost by that single stroke, and found himself embittered by the turn of events. At the same time, he had introduced himself to the world of high-pressure tournament golf. He had made an impact far-reaching in its effects, for now the boy—he was then 25, and relatively unknown—was regarded as a possible new superstar. He could not know what strange quirks fortune had placed in his future, what obstacles he was going to have to endure.

A newspaper man who covered that 1964 Open remembers well the inherent drama built around Venturi's comeback, the heat wave, the stirring charge at the end and the emergency conditions that prevailed in the form of a doctor following him around the course. The USGA has always been firm in its stand that no golfer shall receive any aid or comfort while actively engaged in a championship tournament. The fact that Venturi did receive such aid, with the tacit approval of Joe Dey, the USGA's executive director, added to the uniqueness of the situation.

"He looked absolutely terrible," the man recalls. "He was pale and shaky. It seemed as though his legs would not move properly. We thought, several times during those final eighteen holes, that he was going to fall. It seemed an effort for him to put one foot in front of the other and make himself follow the ball. It was the gutsiest performance I've ever seen, and I wonder why his golf didn't suffer."

Venturi drew millions of printed words of praise for his victory and his great courage. He became the sentimental favorite of many, and he responded with sincerity and thank-fulness to the thousands of congratulatory letters and tele-grams that were sent to him by fans from all parts of the country.

After the tournament, he made known a telegram he had received at its onset, from a parish priest in San Francisco who had established a close relationship with him.

It was a six-page document, most of it personal and undis-closed, but the part that Venturi felt would contribute to the rallying of others who were depressed read this way:

> Keep your composure. Never let anything great that hap-pens to you get you too elated. Never let anything bad get you down. Ask that the Lord let you play to the best of your ability. You are truly the new Ken Venturi, born out of suffering and turmoil but now wise and mature and battle-seasoned.

Venturi tried to explain how much the words from Father Francis Kevin Murray had helped, but he felt he could not properly give justice to the inspirational missive.

"All I can say," he concluded lamely, "is that I knew I had a friend out there somewhere. I knew somebody was really rooting for me, really pulling for me to do my best. It helped. Boy, did it ever help."

Venturi's wife, Conni, herself such an integral part of Ken's ordeals, was, of course, a daily spectator at the tournament. She was tearful at the finish, both in joy for the small miracle her husband was working and at the concern she felt for him during the heat exhaustion.

"All I can remember thinking during those final holes," she recalled to a sports columnist, "was how very much Ken deserved what was happening. After all the troubles and all the disappointment, he was finally on top of his world. It was our great moment, believe me. I can remember when he won a small check after one of his comebacks, in a tournament on the east coast somewhere. He called me to tell me about it—and started crying on the phone. But when a man gets so involved in something, as Ken is in golf, small gains like that mean a great deal."

The drama and excitement of Venturi's victory was one thing; the consequences for the USGA was another. Finally having been made aware of the seriousness of the situation, the group had decided, in a rather history-making decision, to spread the tournament out over four days instead of the traditional three, with the final thirty-six holes jammed into the third day. The opponents of the double round, who for years had argued that forcing a man to endure that could only hurt the golfing quality, now had a strong point. They pointed to Venturi's heroic finish, and insisted that he could have become seriously ill from the effects of his burden.

It was done, and although Venturi did not present a threat in the 1965 Open played at the Bellerive Country Club in St. Louis, Gary Player winning with a 282 and a three-stroke victory over Kel Nagle in an eighteen-hole playoff the following day, it was Venturi who had changed a long-standing tradition. And it has been, in all honesty, a change for the better. The tournament can now be played as a true test of golf and at a reasonable pace, with undue stamina no longer a prerequisite.

CHAPTER EIGHT

The Ladies Play

WOMEN'S GOLF HAS HAD ITS GREAT STARS AND ITS GREAT moments, and both deserve treatment in a book of this kind.

A brief listing of the outstanding women golfers, past and present, would include Babe Zaharias, Mickey Wright, Louise Suggs, Patty Berg, Betsy Rawls, and Kathy Whitworth. Among them, these half dozen ladies own most of the LPGA records. They have won more tournaments than any other women, with lower scores and by wider margins. And they have been responsible for some of the greatest moments in women's golf.

The outstanding events, memorable for their dramatic impact, include 1947, when Babe Zaharias became the first American to win the British Women's Open; 1952, when Louise Suggs set a U.S. Women's Open scoring record of 284; 1959, when Betsy Rawls became the first woman to win ten tournaments in a single year; 1961, when Mickey Wright completed a rare sweep of the Women's Open, the LPGA, and the Titleholders championships; and 1969, when Kathy Whitworth won four consecutive tournaments in the span of five weeks.

To start with the ladies means to begin with Mildred Didrickson Zaharias—the Babe.

Born in Port Arthur, Texas, the daughter of a retired Norwegian ship's carpenter, the Babe died in 1956, a victim of cancer at the age of 42. But into her relatively short life span she crammed more glamor, glory, and sports excitement than most people—men or women.

In 1932, she entered the National AAU Women's Track and Field Meet, which that year doubled as the Olympic Trials. She entered eight events, and her performance as a one-woman whirlwind from Texas caught the nation's attention.

The Babe won the 80-meter hurdles, the baseball throw, the shot put, the broad jump, and the javelin throw; she was runnerup in the high jump and fourth in the discus throw. She earned an Olympic Team berth, naturally, and went to the Olympic Games in Los Angeles to become a national heroine.

There she took gold medals in the 80-meter hurdles and the javelin throw; she tied for a gold medal in the high jump but was later disqualified for leaping over the bar head-first— a technique currently the common one among high jumpers. The nation of the early 1930's was hungry for such a girl, for such a larger-than-life release from the Depression Era, and she became the equal of the day's male giants like Babe Ruth and Jack Dempsey. Shortly after her Olympic feats she turned professional, signing for $3,500 a week with a promoter who utilized her myriad talents on a touring road show.

Her accomplishments were many. She once pitched an inning against the Philadelphia Phillies as a temporary member of the Brooklyn Dodgers. She struck out Joe DiMaggio on another occasion.

She worked out with the Southern Methodist University football team, won a fly-casting contest, and finally established herself as the single outstanding female in such diverse sports as softball, bowling, and swimming.

And then she found golf. "I want to be the best woman golfer in the world," she said, and made her professional appearance a memorable one. It was the first time she had ever swung a club, and at the Brentwood Country Club in Santa

Monica, California, she shot a nine-hole round of 43. Babe soon became an awesome driver, booming 250-yard tee shots that easily outdistanced many of the longest male hitters.

In 1946, having applied for readmission as an amateur and having been accepted as such by the USGA, Women's Division, she entered the Women's Amateur championship at the Southern Hills Country Club in Tulsa, Oklahoma. It was a formidable field, replete with the top names of the day such as Maureen Orcutt, Helen Sigel, Louise Suggs, Mrs. Bettye White, and Mrs. Clara Sherman.

Guess who won? You're right. The Babe.

In the first round, she took a 4 and 3 victory over Peggy Kirk. Then she beat Betty Jean Rucker, 4 and 3. A crucial match with Miss Orcutt proved to be no problem at all, the Babe taking a 5 and 4 victory. Now, matched with Miss Sigel, the Babe turned it on, winning 5 and 4 and advancing to the championship round, a 36-hole test against Mrs. Sherman. It was no contest. The Babe won it by the devastating score of 11 and 9.

There was no stopping her after that. Her husband, George Zaharias, an independently wealthy former professional wrestler, convinced her to remain on the tour, and during 1946 and 1947 the Babe won fifteen consecutive tournament victories, including the British Ladies Open played at the Gullane course in Scotland. And it was an impressive victory. She sped through the first four rounds, never forced to play beyond the sixteenth hole. In the semifinals, she crushed the Scottish champion, Jean Donald, 7 and 5. And the championship round was a riot, as she won five of the first six holes in the afternoon eighteen, included an eagle later at the twentieth, and outdistanced Jacqueline Gordon, 5 and 4.

Mrs. Zaharias later signed a contract to do movie shorts for $300,000, and was a personal friend of former President Eisenhower. When she died in 1956, the golfing world mourned. She had been the first true superstar woman golfer, responsible for the surge of fresh interest that has led to today's brilliant female players.

In 1954, while playing in the U.S. Women's Open at the Salem Country Club in Peabody, Massachusetts, the Babe spied a young girl whose long drives and powerful irons caught her eye. The Babe won that Open—her third—but long after spoke of the potential in that young girl, Mickey Wright.

It was Mickey Wright who was to become the "new Babe," while the original Babe continued to play, almost up to the time of her death. Her final record stands as a tribute to all women golfers. She won the U.S. Women's Amateur in 1946, the British Open in 1947, the U.S. Woman's Open in 1948, 1950, and 1954, the Titleholders in 1947, 1950, and 1952, the Vare Trophy for lowest average score for the year in 1954; she was the leading money winner in 1948, 1949, 1950, and 1951, and was made an original member of the Women's Golf Hall of Fame in 1951.

Mickey Wright, born in San Diego, California, in 1935, is now the woman with the most pro tournament victories (81 through 1969), and won her first two major tournaments in 1958, her fourth year as a professional. That season brought to her display case the trophies for victory in the Ladies PGA and the U.S. Women's Open. Three years after that she executed her sweep of the PGA, the Open, and the Titleholders.

She has to her credit, furthermore, the women's record for most birdies shot in an eighteen-hole round—nine—during the Tall City Open in Midland, Texas, when she shot a nine-under-par 62 round. She twice won four consecutive tournaments, in 1962 and 1963. And she shares the record for the widest margin of victory—a twelve-stroke decision in the 1960 Memphis Open.

In 1963, Miss Wright won 13 of the 28 official tournaments she chose to enter, thereby breaking the record of ten she held with Betsy Rawls. Furthermore, in those 28 tournaments, she finished in the top five 24 times and missed the top ten just once. Her earnings produced a sum of $31,269, and it was the first time a woman had gone past the $30,000 barrier. She won the Vare Trophy with a 72.8 average eighteen-hole round and thirteen times broke into the 60's, her best score being a 67 at Dallas. She registered two holes-in-one and a double-eagle on a 480-yard, par-five hole at the Ogden (Utah) Country Club. Later, in 1963, she was named Woman Athlete of the Year as well as being voted into the Ladies Golf Hall of Fame, the last woman to be so honored.

Very few tournaments and almost no honors escaped the girl who drove as far as the men, and her accomplishments have been set up as goals for all those who followed. But, by being compared to Mrs. Zaharias, Mickey Wright was more than flattered. She was embarrassed.

"I don't think that's fair," she said. "Mrs. Zaharias was in a class by herself. As for me, I prefer just being Mickey Wright, and I want to become the best woman golfer in the world." However, in 1965, having been disturbed several times by ulcers, she decided to abandon the tour, leaving behind her records that may never be equalled.

Perhaps her greatest achievement was winning each of the three most coveted championships in women's golf—the U.S. Open, the PGA and the Vare Trophy—four times.

If 1963 was Mickey Wright's year, then 1949 and 1952 belonged to Louise Suggs. She won the U.S. Open in 1949 by an incredible fourteen strokes, with Mrs. Zaharias a distant second. In 1952, at the Bala Golf Club in Philadelphia, Miss Suggs slugged the ball at a record clip, breaking all tournament records with her four-round total of 284, finishing seven strokes ahead of the two runners-up, Marlene Bauer and Betty Jameson.

Miss Suggs, who turned professional in 1948, is the only woman voted to the State of Georgia Sports Hall of Fame, an honor she received in 1966. She won the Open in 1949, and was a four-time runnerup, twice losing to Mickey Wright. She also won the LPGA title in 1957 and three times finished second in that event—all three times losing to Mickey Wright.

Patty Berg, who was to be instrumental in founding the LPGA in 1949, became a professional golfer in 1940, after having won the Women's Amateur in 1938 (by a 6 and 5 score over Mrs. Julius Page) and was runnerup in 1935 (at the age of 17) and 1937. She won the first Women's Open, played in 1946 at the Spokane (Washington) Country Club, 5 and 4 over Betty Jameson, after also having won the medal in that event with a two-round total of 73-72—145. She was runner-up in the Open in 1957, finishing six strokes behind Miss Rawls.

Miss Berg became Babe Zaharias's closest friend, and often her closest golfing rival as well. She won more tournaments (combined amateur and professional) during her career than any woman—83. She added seven Titleholders (the equivalent of the Masters) to her record, as well as seven Western Opens and four World's Championships played at the Tam O'Shanter course in Chicago. Three times she won the Vare Trophy —1953, 1955, and 1956—and was the leading money winner in 1954, 1955, and 1957.

Today's women hit the ball further than any have done in the past. They are more meticulous than their predecessors, and their scores are much lower than those racked up by yesterday's greats. And perhaps the best of today's new breed is Kathy Whitworth, born in 1939 in Monahans, Texas.

Most records have fallen to this young woman who seems destined to become the next member of the Ladies Golf Hall of Fame. She has been a professional since 1958 and it did not take long before she became one of the professionals' finest players.

In 1960, having been on the tour only two years, she won the Most Improved Pro Award, as she did in 1961 after annexing three major tournaments including the U.S. Ladies' Open. The following year she really orbited, winning eight tournaments. One victory in 1964, in addition to several high finishes, preceded a banner year in 1965, when she won eight big ones, the Vare Trophy, the Associated Press designation as Woman Athlete of the Year, and $28,658—the top women's money-earnings figure for the year.

She has yet to be stopped. The next year, 1966, she took home nine individual trophies as well as the Vare, again, and another leading money-winnings total of $33,517. In 1967 eight more tournaments and the Vare Trophy were hers, as was the top money figure for the third year in a row—$32,037.

In 1968 she won eleven tournaments, was named Pro Player of the Year, and established an all-time money winnings record of $48,379 in official earnings (a figure since broken by Carol Mann in 1969). But, by adding her one victory in an unofficial tournament and the purse that went with it, her winnings for the year came to $59,097—the best by far.

But 1969 really belonged to Kathy Whitworth. She entered 28 tournaments and was out of the top 10 only once while winning seven. And four of them came in a row, equalling a feat twice registered by Mickey Wright. It was a tough accomplishment, considering the added pressure of the growing number of improved women players.

Kathy's string started with the Orange Blossom Open in St. Petersburg, Florida, on March 13. She shot rounds of 74, 70, and 72 in the three-day tournament, good for a one-stroke victory over Marlene Hagge and a winner's purse of $2,250.

Moving up the coast, she next played in the Port Charlotte Invitational a week later, and her three rounds of 72, 72, and 74 gave her a 218 that beat Sandra Post by one stroke. The prize money for that one was $2,250 again.

Number Three was the Port Malabar Invitational, held on March 27-March 30, and three rounds of 68, 72, and 70 were sufficient for a four-stroke victory over Mickey Wright and

Francis Ouimet stands between Britishers Harry Vardon and Ted Ray. On September 20, 1913 Frankie made golfing history as he beat the greats and captured the U.S. Open at The Country Club in Brookline, Mass.

Harry Vardon, brilliant British golfer and shotmaker, checks his lie before taking a stroke in 1927 British Open.

Gene Sarazen reflects his own pose in this portrait of himself hanging at Golf House in New York. Photo was taken in 1960. Sarazen, at that time, said he didn't consider his double eagle in the 1935 Masters to be his greatest achievement.

Bobby Jones tried to stage a comeback at the Masters Tournament in Augusta, Ga., in March, 1934. Walter Hagen (white sweater) looks on.

Spectators press around Sam Snead as he plays from sand trap
on Lochgreen Course at Troon, Scotland, in British Open in 1962.

Bobby Jones (center), president of the Augusta (Ga.) National Golf Club, congratulates Ben Hogan (left), winner of the 1953 Masters. Ed (Porky) Oliver was runner-up.

The winners of golf's two major titles—Tony Lema and Arnold Palmer getting ready for the 36-hole World Series of Golf at the Firestone Country Club in Akron, Ohio, in 1964.

Jack Nicklaus won the $125,000 Whitemarsh Open Golf Tournament in Whitemarsh, Pa., on July 6, 1964. He beat Gary Player by one stroke. He missed eighteen-foot putt on the 18th green.

Ken Venturi makes iron shot on the 17th fairway
during the 1956 Masters at Augusta, Ga. He shot
an 80 on the 4th day and blew the tournament.

Mildred Didrickson Zaharias—the Babe—one of the greatest American women golfers—being bussed happily by her husband after another tournament victory.

Patty Berg in the 1956 women's pro division of the All American Golf Tournament at Tam O'Shanter golf club at Chicago, Ill., makes a tough shot from the pavement onto the green.

Kathy Whitworth blasts out of a sand trap during the final round of 1966 Women's Titleholders Golf Tournament which she won at Augusta, Ga.

Charles Sifford, a leading black golf pro, puffs a big cigar as he putts during a round of the 1968 Cajun Classic at Lafayette, La. The cigar is his trademark.

Gary Player of South Africa prepares to putt in the $100,000 Greater Milwaukee Open in 1969. He finished the round six strokes off the pace.

Four golfing greats—Jimmy Demaret, Jack Burke, Ben Hogan, and Sam Snead—gather around the trophy to the winner of the Ninth Annual Palm Beach Round Robin tourney at the Wykagyl Country Club, New Rochelle, N.Y., in June of 1950.

The Big Three of Golf in 1968—Player, Palmer, and Nicklaus—competing in the Big Three Golf 72-hole competition. Photo was taken at Dorado Beach, Puerto Rico.

$2,625 in winnings. Finally, with the record-equalling opportunity staring her in the face, she entered as the favorite in the Lady Carling Open in Palmetto, Georgia.

It is a prized tournament, and all the best women golfers in the country were there—including Mickey Wright. But Kathy was equal to the demands of the course and the press of the crowds, and she carved out rounds of 70, 72, and 70 for a 212. Yet she could not shake the dogged Miss Wright, who finished with an equally torrid 212. They went into sudden death—and Kathy won it on the first extra hole, taking away the tournament and the $2,625 in prize money.

It had been a satisfying month, with four straight tournament victories and $9,750 in earnings!

Kathy went on in 1969 to capture the Patty Berg Classic with a 69-73-72 total of 214; the Wendell-Western Open with a 69-72-72 total for 213, and the River Plantation Open in Conroe, Texas, with a 70-71-72 aggregate of 213. Her winnings for the year came to $48,971, a scant $181 short of another leading figure, that distinction falling to Carol Mann with $49,152.

But if Kathy Whitworth is the recognized queen of modern golf, there are several women who are ladies-in-waiting. Carol Mann, of course, is the chief rival, and also included are such female stars as Sandra Haynie, Sandra Post, JoAnne Gunderson Carner, Clifford Ann Creed, Shirley Englehorn, Cathy Lacoste, Susie Berning, Margie Masters, and Marilynn Smith.

Much has been made of the difference between the men and the women with respect to golfing abilities. Certain points are clear and nearly irrefutable. For instance, the men, generally, hit a longer ball. They have more strength for their drives and more stamina for the demanding rigors of tournament play.

In deference to these basic inequalities, a few specific advantages are offered to women golfers. They drive off from tees that are situated nearer to the greens, and their tournaments, for the most part, are completed with three rounds. Their scores are usually higher than those of their male colleagues, and they are at a distinct disadvantage when attempting to compete with the men on an equal golf footing.

In the summer of 1970, as part of a promotional exhibition of golf at a New York State resort hotel, Doug Sanders and Carol Mann were matched in an eighteen-hole challenge round. Sanders was forced to use the men's tees while Miss Mann was allowed to tee up from the shorter ladies' markers. Sanders beat her by a dozen strokes, and afterwards, Miss Mann admitted that, at least in golf, the Women's Liberation Movement is doomed.

"We (the women) cannot compete with the men on the course. They drive much too far, their iron shots are greater in distance, and they are more equipped to handle a golf course physically. I would like to see mixed doubles tournaments, however, such as the tennis people conduct. I think it would make for a greater fan interest and would add some spice to the tour."

Women have been playing golf as long as the men, if not with as much dramatic success. Records show that when John T. Reid, generally acknowledged as the Father of American Golf, first teed up on a converted cow pasture in Yonkers, N.Y., his playing companions were John P. Upham, Mrs. Reid, and another woman, Carrie Low. The date was March 30, 1889.

Gradually, women accepted the sport as one in which they could participate, and they began to follow suit to their British counterparts, who had been playing competitively for a much longer period of time. As the game took hold with American girls, the British slowly began to lose their clear-cut superiority, as reflected in Babe Zaharias' British Open victory of 1946 and the swing in favor of the American girls in the more recent Curtis Cup matches.

The women's game never caught on with the same degree of rabid interest as the men's, because most golf addicts are anxious to gasp at and admire booming tee shots. The women, not capable of such long hitting prowess, are forced to make up for their lack of distance with extra iron and chip shots, and this produces a blasé effect on the spectators—most of whom are men and many of whom are seeking pointers for their own game.

Nonetheless, women play their unique brand of quality golf, and there are, suddenly, more and more teen-age girls seeking entry into this glamorous world.

Today's women golfers on the professional tour are no longer treated with second-hand courtesy. They are wooed and pursued, as they say, and their tournaments—particularly the more prestigious ones—are razor-sharp display cases for their talents. The purse money is going up as well, and as long as women such as Kathy Whitworth and Carol Mann can earn nearly $50,000 in a single year from golf purses alone, there is the promise of rapid growth for the future.

Perhaps the idea of mixed doubles will catch on. It seems worthy of consideration, either as a match-play event, best-ball, or individual scoring competition. As Carol Mann has suggested, the tennis people have been singularly successful in bringing this type of attraction to the sports world they inhabit, and tennis experts universally agree that a good male star could easily dominate any of the outstanding women players.

Unfortunately, the image of the woman golfer is still largely confined to the country club set, to those circles of women who can afford the afternoons, the expense, and the luxury of someone else minding the children and cleaning the house. But a visit to any public course will quickly dispel such thoughts, for there are thousands of young girls and women playing golf, for whatever reason and motivation.

Women also have been in much greater evidence as part of tournament galleries—young women who study the players for tips and pointers as well as watch with admiration. The women struck a great blow for their cause when they switched to the comfortable Bermuda shorts instead of the traditional long skirts, for aside from the visual delights, which are nothing to scoff at, they have provided a practical approach to improving their game.

A man recalls bumping into Doug Sanders a few years back in the dining room of the Sheraton-West Hotel in Los Angeles. He was sitting with Dave Marr and they were naturally discussing golf. The topic gradually shifted to the women on the tour, to the small-time purses, and the second-citizen sort of treatment the ladies drew from the golfing public as a whole.

"It's just not right," Sanders said. "Some of those women play as well as anyone. Besides, if you look at the weekend tournaments at courses throughout the country, you'll find as many women playing as men. If there is all that much of an interest, they'll keep getting better and better. It happened in men's golf, when the kids became addicted to the game. And it will happen with the girls, too, bless 'em."

Club pros—working pros who teach and instruct rather than chase after the pot of gold on the tour—will say they are giving as many lessons to women as to men. They will further admit that the caliber of the women, as golfers, is improving each year. They do foresee the day when women will be able to play on a par with the men, however remote the thought may seem to the more entrenched chauvinists.

"For the women," says one pro, "the secret will be in their irons and approach shots. If they cannot match the men in strength off the tee, there is no reason why they can't match them in precision chipping. Driving 250 yards is not really necessary if the irons are good. Look at some of the less rugged men players, such as Gary Player. He was never a long hitter, but his game on the fairway is perhaps second to none."

Finally, the urge to compete will blossom so long as the prestige for women golfers grows. The distinction of winning —indeed, of even gaining entrance to—such tournaments as the U.S. Women's Open, the LPGA, the Titleholders, and several of the more lucrative tournaments should continue to work its attraction on the women stars of the future.

"How did it go today, dear?" a husband might one day ask.

"Fine. I broke eighty. How was your day at the office?"

It's coming, men. And be glad of it.

CHAPTER NINE

The Color Line Is Broken

CHARLIE SIFFORD IS A PIONEER. HE MAY NOT HAVE REAL-
ized it, and he might not have intended it, and he most certainly does not want it. But he cannot escape the distinction.

Charlie Sifford is black. He is also a professional golfer,
one of the few blacks to claim that identity. In fact, the word
identity has become an important part of Charlie Sifford's
world, because he earned it in an atmosphere undeniably difficult, in a world not made for him but one he chose to enter.

Charlie Sifford is as much a man of courage as the Blacks
who have achieved so much in other areas of American so-
ciety and its changing structures. He is a golf pro, a master
player, and he must be set apart in order to define the Great
Moment in Golf he created. Only in his case, it is more than
a great moment. It is more meaningful, more significant than
a single tournament or a single shot.

To place into perspective the value of Charlie Sifford to the
world of the professionals' tour a bit of history, not only of
golf but of the nation, is necessary.

When golf became the vogue in America, its greatest in-
roads were made at the country clubs and the private golf
clubs—areas not part of the world of the southern-born black.
But the game itself, not its spin-off effects, attracted a young
man from Charlotte, North Carolina. He wanted to be a
golfer, and it was an unlikely desire, indeed, for a person in
his particular circumstances.

No blacks belonged to the country clubs and no blacks
were in evidence along the upper middle class paths across
which the first great golfers traveled. Amateur golfers, in the

beginning, were the only ones treated with the respect and admiration of the golfing public. The pros were often looked upon as shoddy interlopers.

But men with determination and foresight gradually prevailed, and the professionals, largely through the efforts and accomplishments of such great players as Gene Sarazen, Walter Hagen, and Tommy Armour, came to occupy a respected niche in the game.

Not so for the black, who was busily engaged in more basic endeavors, such as searching for adequate housing, education, and employment. Golf was a rich man's game, an idle man's game, a white man's game, if you will allow the generalization. Golf, for the black, was a waste of time.

Not so for Charlie Sifford, who was determined to play the game with the pros and as a pro. He was a good golfer from the beginning, a fact so much more meaningful because he learned the game himself. No pros were engaged in teaching the blacks, and no blacks in Charlotte had the money with which to seek out the teaching pros.

"It was my game from the start," Sifford said once, "and I decided that if I could play it as well as most men, I would try play it with the best. I love the game. The rest? Well, golf is my game as much as it is the game of any other pro. We don't have any trouble, and I do not like to talk about the rest of it. You all have heard the story. It's not my way to spell it out. That's for the other people. I play golf."

Yes, Charlie Sifford does play golf, and in his way he has become a fixture, a familiar face on the tournament trail. He has become known for the ever-present cigar clenched at a jaunty angle in his teeth; for his quick smile and ready friendship; for his cooperation with the press and media; for his insistence that, first and foremost, he is a golfer. But mostly, he has become known to millions as a professional golfer of rare skills, which is all he set out to accomplish in the first place.

Charlie Sifford was born in Charlotte on June 2, 1923. He became a pro in 1947, and only then did he begin to realize the difficult nature of what he had undertaken. His winnings were meager and the tournaments were slow to accept his entry blanks. He was a teaching pro for seven years before his name first appeared on a money-winning list. That was in 1954, when his winnings for the year amounted to $281.43. Not an auspicious start, by any means.

The years lengthened and spread out, and yet the money did not accrue to any appreciable degree. By today's standards, his earnings for 1954 through 1960 are paltry; by the standards then they were equally flimsy. Certainly, they were not sufficient to sustain a single man, and a man with a family was forced to seek other income. This made for greater difficulty in honing a golf game, for constant practice is a necessary requisite to progress in golf.

In 1955, Charlie Sifford earned $1,614. In 1956, $2,328. In 1957, $1,285; 1958, $1,490; 1959, $2,926; 1960, $6,923. It was not until 1960 that Sifford was ranked at all among the American money-winners, and his rank that year was 51st.

Indeed, he has never been ranked any higher than 25th (in 1967, when he earned $47,025, his highest total to date), But, like other pros such as Mason Rudolph, the Hebert brothers, Lionel and Jay, and Bobby Nichols, Sifford has been able to earn a comfortable living by finishing high up in the tournament events without actually winning many. His outright victories number only four—one in 1957, one in 1963, one in 1967, and another in 1969. Yet his earnings, since 1962, have never dropped below $12,639 in any year, and have not been lower than $33,180 since 1968.

The financial return, however, is not the most important aspect of Sifford's career. His presence on the courses of the country is that, for each time he entered a tournament, another chink in the stone wall was created. He pioneered each time he strode a fairway, each time he was accepted as an entrant. To list each and every accomplishment in terms of "first Negro to play in the so-and-so tournament" is meaningless. Rather, let it be said that Sifford has earned respect as a golfer and as a man.

In 1957, Charlie won his first tournament, the Long Beach Open, but the magnitude of that championship is reflected in his earnings for the entire year—$1,285. He did not win another until 1963, when he came in ahead of the rest of the field in the Puerto Rico Open. That year he was 49th on the money derby list, having won $16,564. His first tournament success of any real consequence, however, came in 1967 when he took the Greater Hartford Open.

It was, of course, the first time a Negro had won the event. To Charlie Sifford, that triumph held even greater significance, for it represented both his biggest personal victory and the largest single check he had pocketed. He values these two factors higher than the "first Negro, etc." because he is that sort of a man.

When he won, when it was over and official, he was a man moved to great emotion. He cried, and the tears, ludicrously, ran down the stump of that ever-present stogie.

"I worked twenty long and hard years for this," he said at the official trophy presentation, as the crowd of 18,000 cheered, for it was indeed a popular victory.

"There were times when I wanted to quit the tour, when it all became too much, both for me because I am a Negro and because of the lack of immediate success. But my wife, Rose, prevailed on me to stick with it.

"I wanted to quit and she told me not to. She said I had put in too much time and too much effort to pack it in now. I'm glad I listened to her. I'm glad for a lot of things, but mostly for Rose. I have a son playing golf at USC and I have another son who won't be a year old for another month yet. That's kind of a new start for us as a family . . . and today is kind of a new start for me as a golfer.

"Now that I've got a little money in my hands, it takes the pressure off winning. I think it will allow me to play better golf, because if you don't worry about winning bread money, you can relax. That just has to help a golfer, being able to afford being relaxed all the time."

Then Charlie Sifford, who had finished eight of his last nine events in the money, accepted a check for $20,000.

Two years later, in a tournament with, perhaps, a bit more prestige, the 1969 Los Angeles Open, he won another $20,000 for his first place finish. But the Greater Hartford was his first, and so it deserves more detailed treatment.

It had been a select field that had started that tournament, one that included most of the big names. Palmer, Nicklaus, and Casper did not enter, but others like Gary Player and Frank Beard, Lee Trevino and Tony Lema, Dave Marr and Tom Weiskopf, Dave Hill and George Archer did. But Sifford's competition came from two young tour members, Steve Oppermann and Terry Dill, plus a veteran player—Doug Ford.

Dill led after three rounds, but faded to a 72 that included five bogeys on Sunday and finished tied for seventh. Oppermann held the lead in the final round, shooting superb golf, until the fourteenth, when Sifford made his move. Predictably, he acted with daring. He drove long and straight off the tee, smacked a solid five-iron to within 75 feet of the cup and then went for broke.

"I know it sounds sort of dumb to say it now," he grinned later, "but I chipped at the hole. I was hoping."

The wild hope suddenly became wilder reality, as he holed out for an eagle-three and took the lead from Oppermann. He played out in par after that, keeping the youngster at bay, and he finished the round with a score of 64, his lowest by five of the four rounds in the tournament. The final eighteen included five birdies and the eagle, and when they turned for home at the tenth, he swung around to his playing partner, Bobby Cole, and said:

"A 31 now will win it, right?"

Cole looked at him strangely. "And you are going to shoot a 31, is that it, Charlie? Good luck, because this is a tough course."

Charlie did come in with 31, on the championship Wethersfield Country Club course, and he won the big tournament. His final score was 272, built on rounds of 69, 70, 69, and 64. It was a 12-under-par performance—masterful golf in anyone's handbook.

The come-from-behind victory was not certified until the eighteenth had been played by Ford, who had an outside chance if he could get an eagle-two on the par-four final hole. It is unlikely but possible, on the compact Wethersfield course, much more likely than on other courses. Doug knew his chances, since he was playing three threesomes behind Sifford, and he went for the big one. But his tee shot hooked to the left into rough, and he emerged with a par that took him out of contention.

Oppermann finished a stroke back, settling for $8,000 less than Charlie's $20,000 bonanza.

It was a good year for Sifford. Prior to the Hartford, he had finished fifth in the Greensboro Open, sixth in the Dallas Open and tied for tenth in the Canada Open. His earnings for the year, as stated earlier, was a personal high of $47,025.

Sifford, who took to golf as a youngster, received his first contact as a caddy at the Carolina Country Club in Charleston, South Carolina. He earned thirty-five cents a round.

When his family moved to Philadelphia, he continued his relationship with golf by caddying and playing on public courses, in addition to becoming an amateur welterweight prize fighter. Then he moved to the West Coast, established residence in Los Angeles, and played his golf at the Cobbs'

Creek Course, a public establishment. It was there that he became friendly with the famed singer Billy Eckstine who, in effect, sponsored him for seven years by retaining him as his personal teaching pro.

"Billy's a good golfer," Sifford grins, "but he still gets angry whenever I beat him. Honest to God, I owe that man a lot. The money I made kept us going until the tour became successful for me. Without his help–and often it was more than financial help–I would have had to drop out. I would have had to give up golf in order to support my family."

Playing as an "unattached" golfer, which means from a public course, Charlie entered his first U.S. Open in 1959 and finished well back of the ultimate winner, Billy Casper. A return engagement in 1960, when Arnold Palmer won the championship, met with the same meager success, as Charlie shot a 297 and won $260 while finishing 17 strokes off the pace. The only tangible advancement was in his winnings–he had taken home $240 in 1959, with a score of 299.

The Los Angeles Open of 1969, played at the Rancho Park Municipal Golf Club, provided Sifford with icing on his particular Satisfaction Cake. Casper was the defending champion and was entered again, but neither his presence nor that of the other titans–the Palmers, the Nicklauses, the rest–made any difference to Sifford.

"Like I said," he stated after winning. "With a little cash around the house, the pressure is off. It's easier to win, because it's easier to play relaxed golf. I always knew it would be that way, but there wasn't a heck of a lot I could do to get there except start winning, and I wasn't a good enough golfer to win much when I was younger. I'm just fortunate to have gotten my game in shape before I got too old to play."

Sifford's victories, which came relatively late in his career, heartened those who had come to revere the middle-aged representatives of the tour who continued to win and show consistent abilities. They were Ben Hogan and Sam Snead,

Julius Boros and Dr. Cary Middlecoff. And now they were able to add Charlie Sifford's name to the list—yet another list on which he was the first of his race.

The color line is fully broken now. There are no longer many—if any—barriers that face a black golfer. It is true that Sifford, despite his record, has not yet been invited to play in a Masters Tournament, but with current sentiments the way they are among his fellow pros, that should soon change. The Masters management is permitted to pick a maximum of a dozen golfers as "special invitees" and there has been some mystery as to why Sifford has not been one of those so selected, since some of those who were exhibited portfolios not quite as impressive.

Perhaps, for the tour golfer, the question of where to go off the course is accentuated for the Negro, but this hardly represents a major dilemma any longer. And there are young blacks on the tour today—both men and women—who are determined to play the game for its sake and prove themselves on the course, where they feel action will speak far louder and with far more significance than rhetoric.

What Charlie Sifford has done for the Negro tour pro is impossible to fully estimate. He took the brunt of the early trouble for them, showed the way, blazed the trail, opened the doors. His acceptance on the tour was a major breakthrough. It cannot be minimized, for golf today occupies a high place in the country's sports framework and any reflection on the game is a mirror image of the nation's socioeconomic patterns.

By that, it should become clear that Sifford has shown young blacks how to earn big money in yet another field. And he has shown them something of far greater import—that perseverance and dedication can overcome what words or violence cannot.

"If I was to give any advice," Sifford says, "and I don't like to, as a rule, because what's good for me may not be good for anyone else, I would tell the kids to take up golf because it is a game, a sport, and not a crusade. There is nothing to make right, no injustice to be settled, no wars to win aside from the tournament wars that go on almost every week. People say there is nothing like competition in sports to make everyone equal, and it's true. If I'm leading a tournament, there are fifty guys after me because they want to win, and for no other reason.

"It was rough for me, but I never undertook the job because I felt it was anything more than the way I wanted to earn my money and spend my life. I accepted whatever it was that came along early, and I'm accepting things still. If I haven't won many tournaments, that's my fault. But no one has prevented me from playing in them, especially today. That's all I can ask, and I guess that's all anybody can ask. Just to get the opportunity. That's it."

Sifford must rank, however, with Jackie Robinson, who broke baseball's color line and who tolerated and absorbed much more trouble and abuse than any man should expect to encounter before he is accepted as part of a game. Robinson was an instant success which, perhaps, made it a bit easier, though he denies that. Sifford was not an immediate smash, and the years of struggle must have seemed even more unbearable because of it.

In addition, just as black youngsters are taking up tennis today, at the urging of such stars as Arthur Ashe, they are beginning to discover golf. The public courses are packed with youngsters of all colors, all believing they are new Palmers, new Caspers. And new Siffords, too.

"I guess I am looked up to by the Negro kids," Sifford admits. "I don't know, but I guess it would be a natural thing. I'll do whatever I can to help, to teach. But if I know kids, they won't need me for too long. They'll be better than I ever was before they're twenty. Palmer kept raving about Nicklaus when Jack first turned pro. He said he had never seen anyone hit a ball so hard or so far. But Jack had been playing since he was ten, so it figured he'd be pretty good by the time he was in his early twenties.

"Anytime the kids pick up a game, they make it better because they have more time to play it, to practice it, before they compete on a major level. It's the same with golf, no matter what color a kid is. They're better today than they were yesterday, and they'll be still better tomorrow. I'd like to watch some of these kids ten years from now. Not play against them, just watch them."

But if some of these kids Charlie Sifford is watching in ten years are Negro, he should know there is at least half a chance they are playing because of what he started, of what he made possible. It should be a nice feeling, for all too few of us have had the opportunity to be pioneers.

CHAPTER TEN

Gary Player and Other Players

THE TOURING PROS OF TODAY ARE, AS A GROUP AND SINGLY, the best golfers the game has yet produced. They are the product of the golf boom of the 1950's when, as youngsters, they were stirred by the names of such stars as Sam Snead and Ben Hogan and others, and began to take an active interest in the sport. Such participation by teen-agers has, in other sports, produced performers who far outdistanced the older heroes, and so has it happened in golf.

The prize money and the glamor attached to the sport acted as the catalyst in sparking the revolution in its interest and growth. Now these younger men are themselves pros, burning up courses and shattering par as no collection of players was ever able to do.

Several outstanding touring pros deserve mention in these pages. Among them are Gary Player, Billy Casper, George Archer, Tony Jacklin, Lee Trevino, Dave Hill, Larry Hinson, Frank Beard, Bruce Crampton, Tom Shaw, Tom Weiskopf, Deane Beman, Dave Stockton, Bob Murphy, Bob Lunn, Dick Lotz, and Bruce Devlin.

This list offers the best of the "older" pros as well as the cream of the newer stars, who have not yet made a shattering impact on the tour but seem destined to wield their influence in the near future.

Gary Player, of course, has ranked with Arnold Palmer and Jack Nicklaus as a reigning member of the Big Three in the early and late 1960's—a Big Three that has since become a Big Four with the inclusion of Billy Casper.

The little South African brought with him from his native

Johannesburg all the needed ingredients for golf stardom—color, personality, immense talent, and a magnetic attraction for the spectators. He ranks sixth on the list of all-time money winners and has to his credit such notable tournament wins as the Masters (1961), the PGA (1962), and the U.S. Open (1965), as well as two British Open crowns (1959 and 1968).

It must be added, however, that the male pros such as Rodriguez still consistently outhit the women drivers, and Chi Chi's case of the "shorts" is not so much in distance but in comparison to the bullyboys, such as Palmer and Nicklaus.

Rodriguez has had to employ infinitely more finesse to his drives, and the distance he gets is credited to his great wrist action, much the same way as Hank Aaron's lightning-quick and powerful swing of a baseball bat.

Born in 1936, Player was the tour's leading money-winner in 1961, when he earned a purse total of $64,540. Since that time he has been a consistent winner, spanning the years 1962 through 1969 with average earnings of $65,000 annually. He is, moreover, only a periodic participant on the tour, preferring long respites at his home in South Africa from the pressure and tension of tournament golf.

Player's philosophy is built around physical fitness, and he has become the leading exponent of the sound body theory on the tour.

"A golfer's scores always seem to go up as he ages," Player has said, "and I see no reason for that to happen. Golf is a game of fractions and inches, and your reflexes must be kept razor-sharp to play winning golf. When a man begins to age, his reflexes start slowing down almost imperceptibly, but if you work hard at maintaining them, you can continue to play top golf."

And that is what Player has always played—top golf. When he won the 1965 Open at the Bellerive Country Club in St. Louis, he donated the prize money of $30,000 to the Caddies' Scholarship Fund. The reasoning behind this unusual and generous gesture? "Golf in the United States has been good to me. I should like to do something good for golf in the United States."

Player has adopted a characteristic all-black golfing uniform which, he says, is merely a matter of personal choice.

"I don't like to be flashy or showy," he states with a smile, "and black is the plainest color I know. My game is golf, not entertainment, and I dress to be comfortable, mentally as well as physically."

Gary's first American tournament championship came in 1958, when he won the Kentucky Derby Open. He had played the tour the year before with only moderate success, winning a total of $3,286, but it was in 1958 that he began to give solid evidence of his very considerable talents.

In 1969, Player finally cracked the $100,000 barrier, but his total of $123,897 was good enough only to gain him fifth place in golfdom's financial standings. Yet he had never played golf so well, and he was as pleased with his consistent sharpness on the courses as he was with the money.

"For a man like me, fitness is the whole story. I can't hit as long as the big men, and my stamina is less than perfect. But I stay in shape and play each shot as if the entire tournament is riding on it."

Player is recognized as a master with the irons and a sure and steady putter, and he is the first to admit he has to make up in accuracy for what he lacks in distance and power.

"He is," says Sam Snead, "perhaps the finest craftsman of us all. He studies the game in such detail that he knows exactly what each shot means to the tournament. Most of us don't have that kind of patience or concentration. We just go out and hit 'em."

Many observers believe that the 1965 Open showed Player at his best, for the course demanded a craftsman and the pressure of the tournament demanded a strong man. Player finished the regulation 72 holes in a tie with another foreigner,

Australian Kel Nagle, with a final score of 282. His four rounds were a study in consistency (70, 70, 71, 71) and overcame brilliant flashes by Nagle as well as Frank Beard. But Nagle's 69 on the final day knotted the tournament, and the 18-hole playoff was scheduled for the following day. It produced another machine-like 71 for Player, while the up-and-down Nagle was down that day and lost by three strokes. Player, forever modest, insists that Nagle played that extra round with a mental burden.

On the fifth tee, with Player ahead by a stroke, Kel hooked his drive into a group of spectators and the ball struck an elderly woman on the forehead. She collapsed to the ground, blood beginning to appear on her head, then lost consciousness.

Nagle was visibly shaken. Player attempted to console him, but the incident took the edge off Nagle's game. In fact, the degree of his agitation soon became evident to everyone.

The ball had bounced about twenty feet away from the fallen woman, and on the very next shot Nagle again drove into a cluster of fans, this time striking another woman on the ankle. The ball caromed into the fairway where Nagle nervously approached it and then dumped his third shot into a trap. He finally took a double-bogey six on the hole and was finished.

Ahead by five strokes, Player continued to play as if he were behind. It was precision golf, unspectacular but flawless.

"I can't change my game to fit the situation in a tournament," he insists. "If I tried to do that, I wouldn't win anything. I am not the greatest golfer in the world, and I cannot afford to take any chances. I guess I'm a conservative."

That is his way, and it consistently pays off. Of all those golfers (eleven) to finish with more than $100,000 in 1969 winnings, only Player competed in fewer than twenty tournaments. He finished in the top five places in ten events, which included a victory in the Tournament of Champions, second place in the PGA, the Colonial National, and the Milwaukee Open, third place in another event, and a tie for third in two others.

If Player is methodical and tries not to attract attention, Lee Trevino is the diametric opposite. The bubbly Mexican-American thrives on fan contact. He is friendly and gregarious and actively seeks out the galleries.

Born in Dallas in 1939, Trevino broke through to a position of national prominence in 1968 when, during his third year on the tour, he took home winnings of $132,127—enough to finish sixth in the financial standings. That year marked his dramatic victory in the U.S. Open (his first tour victory), played at the Oak Hill Country Club in Rochester, New York.

He beat Jack Nicklaus by four strokes, shooting a 275, and overtook Bert Yancey, the third-round leader on the final day. His tournament score was low enough to tie Nicklaus' Open record, which the Golden Bear had established just the year before at Baltusrol in New Jersey. It took quite a show of golf to deny Nicklaus a second consecutive crown, and Trevino produced the necessary excellence.

His victory was the first in any Open built on four successive sub-par rounds (he shot 69-68-69-69). He had entered the final day trailing Yancey by a stroke, 206 to 205, caught the leader on the third hole with a par and was tied again by Yancey on the ninth. And then, on the tenth, he broke open the Open.

He parred the hole while Yancey took a bogey. He dropped in a 35-foot birdie putt on the eleventh and another birdie putt—this one from 25 feet away—on the twelfth. He thus needed only par golf over the last six holes to tie Nicklaus' record score, and made it easily. He was never in trouble.

But a personal insight into the man was made clear to the millions of fans watching on television. It came on the eleventh green. Trevino was playing with Yancey that afternoon, and when they reached the green, Trevino was away and thus had to putt first. Yancey picked up his ball and placed the marker a few inches away, to allow Lee a clear shot. When Trevino holed out, Yancey put his ball down on the marker, which was not the original lie. Such an infraction, had he hit the ball, would have incurred a two-stroke penalty, and had Yancey not realized it and signed his card, he would have been disqualified.

Yancey prepared to hit, only to have Trevino rush up to him and say: "Get your ball back on its original position, Bert." He did, and saved his chances.

"This man," Yancey stated later, "is a marvelous gentleman. He didn't have to do that."

Trevino disagreed. "I wouldn't want to win a tournament that way, and I'm sure Bert wouldn't want it that way either."

Trevino has a happy-go-lucky attitude that encourages fans. He is loose and relaxed—his two favorite words—and never seems to be adversely affected by pressure. It takes a special sort of emotional makeup to go through the continuous tension of the tour that way, but Trevino has the gift.

"I like to have fun," he says, "and I think golf should be played for fun. Of course, the money is great, and I suppose I couldn't afford to play golf if it wasn't for the money. But, first of all, I have to be able to laugh. I enjoy laughing at myself on the course, because every time I find myself getting all worked up about being a stroke or two behind, I remember the years when I had nothing. Then the tournament seems to get back in its proper perspective. If I couldn't have fun, I'd try something else."

Trevino is a distinct, and welcome, change on the tour. Born to a poor family, Trevino became a pro in 1966 and that year earned only $600. An astounding progress chart shows his earnings soaring to $26,472 in 1967, $132,127 in 1968, and $112,418 in 1969.

"I hope I never get to the point where I don't have time for the people," he says. "I never refuse an interview with a news-paperman and I try not to worry about details. I love the travel on the tour, and I can't complain about the food because I remember when we didn't have enough to eat. I don't make an issue of inconveniences, because to me, they aren't.

"I have heard some of the other golfers complaining about the tiny problems, like keeping supplied with clean laundry. Well, maybe they were used to better, but I remember when I had only one shirt and on the day it was being washed I went without one. Golf has been so good to me I won't dare complain. I can't complain, because I had nothing when I started. Everything I have been able to do and everything I have is because of golf.

"If my investments aren't going well, I don't worry about that, either, because the way I started out I never thought I'd have enough money to make investments. I think golf is the greatest thing in the world."

Trevino's charm in public is reflected in the size and decibel volume of his followers.

"I always liked the sound of the phrase 'Arnie's Armies' and I tried to encourage the same kind of support. When it came, we called my galleries 'Lee's Fleas' and I think it's great. If the people stop following you, stop cheering for you, I think you suffer. It's hard to explain, but when I can hear people cheering for me, it gets the adrenalin pumping. I really believe I play better golf."

There is, however, a serious side to Lee Trevino. He lost a close friend when Hawaiian pro Ted Makalena died shortly before the 1968 Hawaiian Open. He immediately entered the tournament and publicly stated: "I want to win this one for Ted."

He did, and when they handed him the winner's check, he handed it to Makalena's widow, with which to start a Ted Makalena, Jr. college scholarship fund.

Attempting to pass off the gesture without fanfare, Trevino spoke seriously about his feelings toward golf.

"I don't want to take everything out of this game. After all it has done for me, I'd like to put something back into it, too. Ted was a good friend and a great golfer. I was grateful to to be able to honor his memory."

Billy Casper spent many of the most fruitful years of his golfing career in the shadow of the Big Three. But he accepts that lack of recognition with typical serenity. "Those other men were the top golfers, and it was only right for them to receive top billing."

Many will argue that statement, for Casper has been, since turning pro in 1955, perhaps the most consistent player on the tour despite several strength-sapping diets necessitated by a highly allergic condition. His strange and exotic foods, ordered for him by a medical specialist, are the talk of the tour, and include such dishes as bear steak, carrot and beet juice, and sesame bread. But seldom have his physical problems interfered with his golf.

Among the many tournaments that bear the name of Billy Casper as their champion are the U.S. Opens of 1959 and 1966, the Bob Hope Classic, the Western Open, the Alcan Tournament, the Los Angeles Open, the Hartford Open, and the Doral Open. In all, Casper has won 41 individual tournaments through the 1969 season, in addition to landing several other accolades.

For instance, he was the leading money winner in 1966 and again in 1968, and he has not been lower than tenth on the money list since the 1957 season. He stands third, behind Palmer and Nicklaus, on the all-time purse-winning list with total earnings of $981,924 through 1969. Five times he has been awarded the Vardon Trophy, a tribute to his consistency since its bestowal is based on the lowest average rounds for a full year. In 1966 Casper was named the PGA Player of the Year.

Casper's most dramatic victory came in the 1966 Open at the Olympia Country Club in San Francisco when, trailing by seven strokes with just nine holes to play, he caught Arnold Palmer, forced an 18-hole playoff and won the championship.

"First place never crosses my mind until the fifteenth hole on Sunday," Casper remembers. "I was playing to hold on to second place until then."

It was on the fifteenth that Casper turned the tables on Palmer and mounted a stirring charge of his own, using Arnie's tactics to demoralize his opponent.

"It seemed every time I looked around, Casper was another stroke closer," Palmer recalls. "I was nervous, and I finally began to wonder on the fifteenth."

Arnie had hooked into the rough and salvaged a bogey-four. Casper, playing with precise determination, sank a fifteen-foot putt for a birdie. Palmer was caught on the seventeenth when Casper pitched from the edge of the fairway to the green and earned a birdie. Palmer took another bogey. Thus, after having lost four strokes on the fifteenth and sixteenth, he found himself in a tie. They played the final hole under excruciating pressure, and both came in with par-fours on the 337-yard eighteenth when they two-putted in, Palmer from forty feet out, Casper from twenty.

The next day's playoff was a replica of the final round. Arnie took an early lead and went two up after five holes when Casper drove into the rough, had to hit out from behind a tree and took a bogey-five. But Billy, serene and confident, came to the eleventh still two strokes behind and ignited again. He sank a 25-foot birdie putt there and another birdie putt of 35 feet on the twelfth to go one up. Palmer had become ensnared in another bogey jinx, picking up four in six holes from the eleventh on, and was never able to catch Casper again. They finished in that order, and Billy Casper was the champion of a tournament he had always held in higher regard than all the rest.

"Is it real?" Casper chortled. "It's like a dream. It's something I've been hoping and praying for, for so long. It's very, very rewarding."

Palmer was still too stunned to speak. He had lost 13 strokes to Casper on the back nine holes in two days. It was traumatic.

"My outlook on golf," Billy says, "is one of thankfulness. Golf has meant more to me than I ever thought it would. It has provided my family with security and a good life, and I am proud to be playing with such people as you find on the tour."

Casper is closely tied to the Church of Jesus Christ of Latter-Day Saints—the Mormon faith—and has always tithed ten per cent of his golf winnings to the church. And his beliefs have colored his entire life.

"There are only four interests that occupy me," he says. "They are religion, family, golf, and fishing, in that order. And when you think about it, the first two are the same. They are two sides to one coin. I don't know what I would have been doing if I had not been able to play golf, but I am absolutely sure that my family and my religion would have meant as much. I don't think there is anything else left for a man, if he has his family and his religion."

Casper has indicated that his golfing victories are affected by his religion.

"If I come in second," he says, as he did in the 1969 Masters, "I'm proud to have finished there. It's just another experience in life. You have to learn how to lose as well as win, and you must try not to be disappointed."

Casper became one of the select few to escalate his winnings past $200,000 in one year, when he earned $205,168 in 1968. And he was thankful for every tournament. "If I win a great deal of money, well, that's great," he says. "But there is also a kind of self-satisfaction that goes with winning, too, and it is as important as the money, believe me."

The part about finishing second and the part about earning a great deal of money fit Frank Beard like a golf glove. In 1968 this free-swinging pro from Dallas, Texas, failed to win a single tournament, yet came away with $101,987 when he counted his earnings at the end of the year.

Indeed, Beard had established a reputation as a never-winner and a consistent earner ever since he started playing top golf, which occurred in 1964, his third year as a professional.

"I don't know why I didn't win any tournaments that year," he states. "In fact, I don't know why some days I can shoot in the sixties and the next day have trouble breaking eighty."

Beard finally began winning steadily in 1969, when he claimed the Minnesota Classic and the Westchester Classic as his own and added second place finishes in the Byron Nelson Classic, the New Orleans Open, the Sahara Invitational, and the Buick Open. He was the nation's leading money winner, earning $175,224.

"Sometimes I try to psych myself in golf," he says. "I'll start a tournament and tell myself 'this is going to be a good round.' So then I'll shoot a 76. The next day, when I feel sorry for myself and depressed in general, I'll show up at the course and go around in 66. Sure, it's puzzling, and if I could put my finger on a reason for the erratic golf I'd probably get rich quick. But I can't, and I have to be thankful for the days when I'm playing well."

Beard's game is marked by his skill as a putter, a fact he characteristictally makes no attempt to hide. "I consider myself one of the three best putters on the tour (the others, in his book, are Dave Stockton and George Archer) and that's where I can make up my strokes. I've never been really satisfied with my drives or my irons, but I have always been able to putt and it keeps me high in a tournament. And before you ask, I don't know why I'm a good putter, either. I never really concentrated on it, any more than on other parts of my game. It just happened, and that's the way it is."

Beard, surprisingly, for an occasional winner, has made golf pay off. He has earned more than $100,000 for three consecutive years (1967, 1968, and 1969) and has not been out of the top fifteen money winners since 1965.

Beard's inconsistency was marked by his play in the 1965 U.S. Open, won by Gary Player in the playoff with Kel Nagle. Frank opened with a mediocre 74, putting him far back in the standings, but countered the next day with a 69. He followed that with workmanlike rounds of 70 and 71 and was two strokes behind the leaders when it was all over.

Frank has never won one of the big four tournaments in golf—the U.S. Open, the PGA, the Masters, and the British Open. But he has earned the respect of the other pros, the toughest golf critics in the world, and he has made a handsome living from his close-but-no-cigar finishes.

Winning tournaments has not been a problem for young Tony Jacklin, the 26-year-old Englishman who has taken the American tour by surprise. Tony came out of nowhere to win the 1969 British Open by two strokes over Bob Charles with a 280 score. He was among the youngest players to ever capture this ancient tournament, and he was doubly pleased because he is a native Englishman.

But his practical approach to golf would not allow him to accept his success without first giving credit where he felt it was due.

"Playing the American tour," he says, "has helped me immeasurably. Against that kind of competition you have to play your best every day, and doing that sharpens your game as nothing else could."

Jacklin's golfing heroics are, apparently, mainly in his future. "He has," says Palmer, "all the potential to be a great golfer."

But for a three-year pro, Tony has already garnered a fair share of those individual honors. In addition to his British Open title, he claims a triumph in the 1968 Jacksonville Open, a tournament in which he finished with a record score of 15-under par for a 273, overcoming a patented late charge by Palmer to win.

Jacklin is another example of this new breed of golf pros. He discovered the game when he was nine years old, caddying for his father, and he began swinging clubs almost immediately.

He competed in tournaments for other boys his age and won several of them.

"I knew I wanted golf to be my life," he stated recently, "so when I was seventeen I dropped out of school and became a professional. I wouldn't recommend that to boys today, though, because I have discovered that an education is a valuable asset."

Jacklin's experience, for one so young, is enormous. In addition to playing on the tour, he has worked in the pro shops, caddied, studied with the proven stars of the day, and weathered the pressure involved in winning, or simply competing in, major tournaments.

"There is no place like the United States to learn what this game is all about," he adds. "Anyone wanting to become a professional should play with these Americans. They're the best, and therefore they are the best to learn from."

The distinguishing mark of young pro golfers is their inability to hold an early tournament lead. Most of the good players—those who will be the heroes in two or three years—have suffered through the frustration of watching leads evaporate before the onslaught of the seasoned performers.

Larry Hinson, another 26-year-old with a bright future, falls into this category.

Hinson is a six-two stringbean who weighs just 150 pounds, and has been playing professionally on the tour only since 1968.

But he has already won his first tournament—the New Orleans Open of 1969—and his earnings skyrocketed from $3,968 in his first year (1968) to $54,267 for 1969. His victory at New Orleans came just one year after his decision to become a professional and graduation from the Approved Tournament Players school run by the PGA.

Hinson, a native of North Carolina who now makes his home in Douglas, Georgia, overcame a bout with polio which left his left arm paralyzed. But a dedicated program of conditioning and therapy allowed him to leave that handicap in his past, and now he smiles at the recollection of how he spent his youth.

"I broke my left arm three times and my right arm twice," he admits with a wide grin, "trying to prove I was going to be an average boy despite the polio. I had some trouble convincing my parents of that, however. I decided that polio wasn't going to ruin my life. After I was better, I remember being so self-conscious about my arm that I wore a jacket all the time so I could keep the arm in my pocket.

"Then, slowly, I decided I should play games with the rest of the guys. I did, and started getting hurt, but it was worth all the trouble. I think it gave me a better appreciation of my body. I am always trying to stay in shape, and even now I still squeeze those sponge balls to maintain the strength in my hands."

Hinson is a pleasant sight on the course. He winds his long, lean body into a semi-circle, then explodes over the ball, whipping his follow-through with a final flourish. He drives long and high, and has begun to master the approach shots, an area of the game that most newcomers find the most difficult to solve.

"My victory in New Orleans was something special," he says, "and not just for the money. It's important to a young golfer to get that first win. It takes the pressure off, and you realize you can play with the good golfers."

There are others.

George Archer won the 1969 Masters in a stunning upset, and that year he earned $102,707 on the tour. But it was only his second-highest money figure, since the previous year he had taken three championships—the New Orleans Open, the Pensacola Open, and the PGA National Team title (with Bobby Nichols)—and earned a whopping $150,972, a figure that ranked him fourth among all money winners. It was a far cry from his earnings of $14,867 in 1964, his first pro-tour year.

"Winning the Masters is the greatest thing that can happen to any golfer," states the lanky six-foot-six former cowpuncher from Gilroy, California, the tallest player on the tour. "It's almost unthinkable for a man like me. I just play each hole trying to do my best, but I never think my best will be better than anyone else's."

But in the 1969 Masters, his best was better than all the rest —although, admittedly, not by much. Yet even his narrow, one-shot victory over a horse-race pack of four other golfers stands as a remarkable demonstration of courage under intense pressure.

His final score of 281 was a single shot ahead of Billy Casper, George Knudson, and Tom Weiskopf, and two ahead of Charles Coody. Going into the final round, Casper held the lead with 208. Archer was one back. Weiskopf, a towering hitter, and Knudson were at 211.

Coody led after fifteen holes but bogeyed the last three to spoil his chances. Weiskopf stayed close but failed to capture the vital advantage. Knudson, too, was always close but just missing.

And on the fifteenth, Archer's chances almost drowned—literally. He hit his second shot into a water hazard, took a one-stroke penalty and then struck a masterful iron shot that landed within six feet of the cup, from which point he holed out to salvage an unlikely par.

"When I hit that shot into the water," he said later, still visibly stunned, "I felt like jumping in after it."

But he saved the hole and the tournament, and played par golf the rest of the way to take the championship. After he finished, he was still denied the joy of immediate victory because Casper, with a good chance, was still on the course. Archer was in with a 72 and Casper was on eighteen. But Casper hit his second shot, to the green, too hard, and the ball rolled forty feet past the cup. It was Archer's Masters, and he later cracked up the awards ceremony audience by showing his arms, too long for the traditional green blazer of victory, and saying: "I'm really surprised they had a jacket to fit me here."

It was a torrid finish, with five fine pros all within one shot of each other, and the lead, after sixteen holes. But Archer, the top putter on the tour, won it.

"My heart still beats thirty thousand beats a second when I think of it," he smiles. "I got every break I could get."

Archer is conceded to be the finest putter on the tour, being possessed of the impossible-to-learn "feel" older men speak of when discussing the art of putting. "He has a way of always hitting the ball squarely," says a grizzled and envious pro. "I've been trying to get it for years and I'm not even close."

Dave Hill, perhaps the most controversial of the younger golfers, drew a loud round of cheers from the public for speaking his views about the course used for the 1970 U.S. Open in Naskra, Minnesota.

"All they need here is eighty cows for it to be a great

pasture," he complained, "and I know that's going to cost me."

It did—a slap-on-the-wrist fine of $150—but Dave had by then conquered the cow pasture and finished second, for a purse of $15,000. Throughout his career, Hill had been an erratic golfer until he started the 1969 season. Then the 33-year-old found the touch, won three tournaments, placed second in two others, finished third in still another, and claimed earnings of $156,423, second to Frank Beard.

"I am my own worst enemy on the course," he admits. "I have a bad temper and it takes away from the necessary concentration. Everything a golfer does should be technically correct. You can break down a swing into scores of individual motions, and each one must be executed properly. I don't care if I win one tournament or a thousand, so long as I am playing the best golf I can."

Hill's search for perfection paid off in 1969 when, in addition to the prize money, he won the Vardon Trophy for lowest average over the year.

And so golf's new breed of bright young stars has invaded the nation's courses. Par never had a chance, and regular scoring in the 60's should soon become a common accomplishment.

Hagen would have enjoyed watching these golden young men. Think of all the "nice shot, kid" lines he could have used, in envy as much as in jest.